SOLA

Hollywood, McCarthyism,
and a Motherless Childhood Abroad

JULIETTA APPLETON

This book reflects the author's present recollections of experiences over time. Some names and characteristics have been changed, some events have been compressed, and some dialogue has been recreated.

Published by Madame and Daughters Press

www.madameanddaughters.com

To request permissions, please contact the publisher at hello@madameliterary.com

First paperback edition September 2022

Cover artwork by Reny Mia Slay

Cover design by Alex Asher Sears

Text design and composition by Jacqueline Sweet

All photos courtesy of the Author

Library of Congress Control Number: 2022942594

979-8-9862656-0-5 (paperback)

979-8-9862656-1-2 (ebook)

For Greta, who saved my life.

And for John, who showed me how to live it.

sola | soh-lah |
Latin
adjective
1. Stage direction given to an actress entering a scene alone.

PROLOGUE
LIGHTS UP

Beverly Hills, 1954. I was two years old, accompanying my father to Dunhill Tobacconist on Rodeo Drive so he could get his fancy British pipe tobacco. He put me down on the floor while he was purchasing his Charles Leonard custom blend, and I wandered out the door unobserved and into the street. Greta Garbo, in a big floppy hat, scooped me up and brought me back into the shop and asked, "Who does this baby belong to?" My father thought this was a hilarious story, movie star saves kid.

I am not sure it was so funny. We were surrounded by movie stars on account of my parents' work. My father was a screenwriter and worked in film PR. My mother was a talent agent. So, the lesson in the story, as far as I was concerned, was either that I was a slippery little devil or that my father was irresponsible. Not that Greta Garbo was my savior, which really, she was.

My childhood seemed like a wordless place, although it was filled with sounds and scents. I remember the hiss of garden hoses, held by silent Japanese men in khaki shirts and pants and pith helmets, as they washed the fallen leaves of camellias and oleanders off driveways. I remember the *chk-chk-chk* of automatic sprinklers as they stuttered across green lawns. I remember the sound of crickets chirruping in the night as my mother carried me to the car for the drive home from my grandparents' house, the cool evening air perfumed by night-blooming jasmine. But I don't remember many conversations that included me. I was ignored, spoken over, or I was admonished.

I was born on February 29, 1952, by elective cesarean, in Los Angeles, California, which in those days was under the dark cloud of McCarthyism. My father's ties to the Communist Party were never very clear to me. He became a member in the 1930s, I believe, alongside a number of his Hollywood colleagues, but I never heard him speak of those ideals. He lived the good life, as far as I could see. I knew him as a Democrat, and a somewhat progressive one at that, a man who championed labor unions but also bought bespoke tobacco on Rodeo Drive. Today, he would probably be a Bernie Sanders supporter. I could see him helping displaced refugees (just as he did during World War II) and using his PR skills to help Amazon workers trying to unionize. The ideas of Communism and a socialist state that grew in popularity in the 1930s and 1940s seemed to be a dream of a better world that would end monarchies and introduce equality, with organized labor and an end to oppression. But the realities of Communism were devastating and maybe that's why he never spoke of it. The dream was not the reality. And as concerns about un-American activities grew, anyone like my father, anyone with a connection to the Communist Party, was seen as subversive and a threat. My father, subversive? A threat? Un-American? These concepts were foreign to me.

I'm the only child of Charles Leonard Appleton and Betty Raskin Appleton. Sometimes I think being an only child is a good thing, but mostly I wish I had real siblings to share the traumas with, or who might have helped avoid them. Wondering what it would have been like is a stupid and painful guessing game because one can never really know what, if anything, would have been different. Would Charlie have left if Betty had more kids? My father told me more than once that he never wanted me, that it was Betty who wanted a child so desperately she "had her tubes blown open." He also told me that I was "too much" for my mother, who, until she died of a heart attack when I was nine years old, was a very healthy woman. I grew up believing that were it not for the demands of a burdensome little girl, of *this* little girl, she would still be alive to take care of me. Once I became a mother myself, I realized that I had been no more demanding than most children. But my guilt and shame were firmly tethered by then.

My mother was forty-one when I was born, my father fifty-two. My mother's past is more vague to me than my father's. My parents met in 1947 at an acting retreat led by Michael Chekhov at the New Canaan, Connecticut, farm of actress Beatrice Straight. At the time, my mother was a theatrical agent in New York City. Her clients included Peter Falk, Telly Savalas, and Deanna Durbin. I've been told that Danny Kaye (then Kaminsky) proposed to her. I know hardly anything else about her life before me. I've got

3

photos of her on her parents' farm in Mountaindale, New York, in the Catskills, when she was in her teens, with her hair in long corkscrew curls and a burdened look on her face; of her maybe in her twenties or thirties on the deck of a cruise ship, wearing white sailor shorts that fall below her knees, canvas crisscross platform sandals, and a jaunty smile; at her desk in her office, wearing a suit with an elephant pin near her left shoulder, her hair rolled up atop her head and on either side of her face in a popular 1940's style, looking pensively at the camera.

Was she happy? Did she choose to be single until she was thirty-eight? Were her Orthodox Jewish parents upset that she went on a cruise alone? Was it true that she planned to marry a man they did not approve of, so she married my father instead, her second choice? Why did they have such control over her life? And if they did, then why wasn't I raised Jewish like everyone else in my family?

I will never know the answers to these questions. But my guess is that my mother wasn't happy, that she would have been better suited to an era where one could be a mother and have a fulfilling job and not have to put up with the self-aggrandizing, arrogant man who most likely cheated on her. I've heard rumors throughout the years that my father had affairs, that my father and mother had even separated, and that my father threatened to take full custody of me. That makes no sense, given how he treated me after my mother died. But there are no relatives or family friends who can verify any of the rumors.

Some people tell me, to be helpful, that it really doesn't matter, that I should live in the present. But it does matter. Knowing who I am, *why* I am who I am, might help me understand the roots of my fearfulness and insecurity. But all I have to rely on are my own experiences. Glimpses into my parents' lives are through the eyes of others, two dissociations away, and surely not entirely true. So perhaps truth is not the issue but a better understanding of my reactivity. What matters is how I feel and why.

1

GENEALOGY

My dear, he wrote, *I am trying to fathom this morale-destroying*
attack on my psyche
And what's all this about your genealogy?
Who cares?
If you must know the truth,
we have no genealogy
Like animals
we are the issue of sperm let loose inside birth pockets
in a moment of passion

When I first read this
when my father wrote me this letter
I was thirty-two
And I laughed
He was a ridiculous,
cloudy, demented, old man
He was eighty-four
As always
his pockets were empty

But I was angry
He was denying me
MY history
Just like he denied me
his time
his attention
his hand to hold
his money
his love
his compassion

And after telling me, *Who cares?*
he went on for two
single-spaced pages
on his old Smith Corona
the ribbon gappy and faded
letters missing from his words
lines x-ed out
notes handwritten in the margins
He did not appreciate the plundering
of his memories
But he still reached for some of them
The earliest ones

He recalled being saved, twice, from child murder
during the two Kishinev pogroms
1903 and 1905
The Cossacks who drank (heavily, he said) at the inn
next to his grandfather's *kvass* stand
told his mother to hide him
inside goose down pillows
in the attic

And she did

These were the same Cossacks
who slaughtered Jews
who tore babies apart
Did these Cossacks intentionally
pass over pillows?
Or just these pillows,
the Epelbaum pillows?

From Kishinev, Russia
to Bukhovia, Austria
my grandmother
and her three young sons
and baby daughter—
Etta
Fishel, Chaim, Ezriel
and Mariam—
trudged through sleet to cross the border
at Grenitz, he says
Mariam almost froze to death
They stopped to warm her alive again

My aunt Leah was born in Austria
So my grandmother was pregnant on this trek
How long were they there?
He doesn't tell me
Just that our name was changed there
to Apfelbaum
before it was changed
to Appleton
in New York City

9

That his father was a woodcutter
with a red mustache
And his mother's father a vintner
(his grandfather, my great grandfather,
the one who sold *kvass*
in the town square)

That he ate his first banana
on the ship to Ellis Island
That they lived on the Lower East Side
Norfolk Street
and Ludlow Street
and then Suffolk Street
where my aunt Clara was born
and then 113th Street in Harlem
and then Bathgate Avenue in the Bronx
and then 179th and Southern Boulevard in the Bronx

When?
And then what?
Let's say that was 1922
I was born in 1952
That's thirty years of my father's life
and his memories that
I can't find
except for gummy, dusty bits
that he shared three years before he died
in 1986

Then there's hearsay
from relatives and friends
added to my own overcast memories

perhaps scenes my father shared
with me
or with an audience of friends
that I overheard

He, Uncle Ezriel, and their friend Jimmy Cagney
boxing their way home from school every day
the allegiances shifting between
Jews, Irish, and Italians,
all tossing epithets as fast as their punches

Jimmy and my father moving
to Hollywood together
in 1924?
Jimmy boxing with his kangaroo Joey
My dad and Jimmy finding a white hood
under the pillow of a friend of Jimmy's
When?

My dad being crushed like a bug by Hollywood
and choked by his own bitterness
Jimmy finding fame
even if he puked before every live performance

I never met my father's parents
I haven't even seen photographs
Would they have loved me?
What work did they do when they got to New York?
When did they die?
Where are they buried?

All those lives

Whose tendrils touched other lives
and should have touched mine
And those memories
They belong to me too
but I can't find them
Who cares?
I do

2

RED DIAPER BABY

At the time of my birth in 1952, my father worked at Twentieth Century-Fox studio on Pico Boulevard. From 1949 to 1951, he had a two-year stint as the director of national press and publications at the Hubbard Dianetic Research Foundation, working first in Elizabeth, New Jersey, and then in Wichita, Kansas, where I was conceived. The Foundation was on the verge of financial collapse and closed because of bankruptcy in February of 1952, by which time my parents were back in Los Angeles. Following the bankruptcy, it was rebranded as the Hubbard Association of Scientologists International, and Scientology as we know it was born.

I have no idea how sympathetic my father was to Hubbard and his ideas, though I don't think he was a fan of any kind of organized religion. When I was in my teens, Daddy bragged to me that he ghostwrote the book *Dianetics*. I've obtained his Hubbard Dianetic Auditor certificate (dated November 17, 1950) and his 1951 federal withholding statement from the Hubbard Foundation,

Wichita ($4,750, the equivalent of about $52,000 in 2022) and found press materials he wrote, so I know when he worked there. I've also looked through lots of L. Ron Hubbard's FBI files and found Hubbard's own words: "… the 1950 and '51 public relations man, Charles Leonard, registered positive on Communism in the police check at Wichita in or around April of 1951, possibly May." And that was when Hubbard fired him. I will never know how he ended up representing the Foundation, but I can only assume his decades-long career at multiple film studios made him valuable to Hubbard as a press director.

My father spent the Golden Age of Hollywood helming publicity and advertising departments for RKO, Universal, and United Artists. He was also a writer involved with the progressive Hollywood Theatre Alliance, founded by a group of New Yorkers living in Hollywood. He worked with Langston Hughes and Donald Ogden Stewart, and his name was often in the Hollywood trade papers. I think my father thought of himself as a writer who did PR, but he was a PR man who happened to write.

Everything changed while my mother was pregnant with me. On September 18, 1951, screenwriter Martin Berkeley named my father and over 150 others as Communists before a sub-committee of the House Un-American Activities Committee (HUAC). On March 24, 1953, another fellow screenwriter, David Lang, named seventy-five additional names and my father's was one of them.

My father was indeed "crushed like a bug" by McCarthyism and the Hollywood inquisition. He went from being Somebody in Hollywood, with a capital S, to an angry, embittered man who suddenly had to rely on others to get work.

McCarthyism didn't just affect the Hollywood players —the actors, directors, writers, and all the people behind the scenes like my father. It affected the wives and husbands of those named, too, as a whole cadre of people were now jobless or penniless, some living with friends, others leaving the country to live cheaply abroad, or living out of their cars. It also affected children—the red diaper babies as we're called—whose lives were often uprooted by McCarthyism and who sustained the impact of having one's parent (or both parents) suddenly and so publicly deemed un-American. I haven't yet met a fellow red diaper baby whose mother or father was able to parent "normally." Most of the victims of the Hollywood inquisition were hypervigilant parents, constantly worried about the next dragon lying in a dark corner waiting to attack, or else they were so lax they didn't know where their kids were half the time.

My father was lucky to have his publicity job at Twentieth Century-Fox, and I don't know how he got it. Perhaps his friend Jimmy Cagney had helped him, or his friend Bill Sholl over at United Artists. But his past credentials conferred status, so he was able to have a paying job with a regular check and we stayed in our house in Studio City.

When I was young, my father wrote plays that were never performed and made some revisions to the book *To the Actor* (which he wrote for my godfather, Michael Chekhov, in 1953). Chekhov, nephew of Anton and a student of method-acting teacher Konstantin Stanislavski, was an actor, director, and acting teacher whose students included Gregory Peck, Marilyn Monroe, Clint Eastwood, and Ingrid Bergman. To me, he was my Papa Misha. My father also wrote Chekhov's book *To the Director and Play-*

wright, published in 1962, which has never had much success as a textbook, not like *To the Actor*.

One of my earliest childhood memories is of being in a playpen in the center of a courtyard with balconies all around me. Maybe I remember it because I saw a photograph of it, but I don't have the photograph, just the snapshot in my head. It is the first place I ever lived, an apartment on Durant Drive in Beverly Hills. I am standing, gold curls shining (before my hair turned dark brown, around age four), squinting into the sunlight and the plantings and the eyes of two stories' worth of neighbors. My mother is not in this picture. She may have been the photographer, but she is probably upstairs in our apartment. I suppose she figured that the more people who watched me, the better protected I was, that her parenting skills were multiplied. I think of that courtyard and feel exposed and frightened.

We moved to Studio City, California, just over the canyon from Beverly Hills, when I was about two years old. Growing up, I was given the usual childhood warnings—you can play on the lawn, but don't run into the street, a car could hit you; stay away from water, you can fall in and drown; be very careful around fire, it can kill you. But it was my parents and my teachers—people I trusted—who were the actual dangers. My mother's intense devotion to the principles of Austrian mystic and self-proclaimed clairvoyant Rudolf Steiner—founder of anthroposophy and Waldorf education—endangered not only me but eventually her own life as well.

Anthroposophy holds some peculiar tenets, and they seemed even more eccentric in the 1950s. Some ideas—for instance, that food should be bioenergetic, have living forces in it whenever possible—make sense even today. Belief in fairies, the etheric body and the astral body, spiritism, and lots of other occult concepts, run rampant through anthroposophy, but I didn't know any of this stuff as a kid, nor do I understand most of it now, much less want to.

I just knew that my mom bought only fertilized eggs and organic produce at the health food store. She baked her own bread, juiced vegetables (and rarely fruits), and forced me and my father to drink her healthful but foul-tasting blends. She subjected me and my father to coffee enemas whenever we became ill with stomach-related problems.

"No, not in my tushy! Not in my tushy!" I screamed as I ran around the house with her trying to catch me, which she always did. I've drawn a blank on where they were administered, but I think the bathtub as it was the closest, waterproof space near the toilet, in case of accidents. My father didn't scream or complain, yet I can't imagine he was happy about this treatment.

My mother would put socks soaked in milk on my feet to bring down a fever. If I had a sore throat, I got sliced raw onions wrapped around my neck and held by a scarf. My mom also went to a chiropractor, and to a homeopath named Dr. Knauer, and saw psychics, because anthroposophists were into all kinds of ways to connect with the spirit world. My mother attended molybdomancy parties, where she and her friends would get together and melt bits of lead in a teaspoon by holding a match underneath it, pour the liquefied lead into cold water, then guess the future by interpreting the molten shapes. I remember holding the cold, melted lump of lead in my hand and trying to understand what good portent my mother was so giddy about. The irony of the toxic lead and the biodynamic food does not escape me today. Melting lumps of lead was a common New Year's tradition, called Bleigiessen, in Germany. Maybe what I'm remembering is a New Year's Eve among the anthroposophists.

Anthroposophists believe that electric lights negatively affect human carbohydrate and oxygen metabolism, so my mom hated incandescent lights and used candles whenever possible. She put candles on our Christmas tree (this, too, is a German tradition) when everyone else had pretty, colored lights that twinkled or flashed.

I used to lie awake and worry that our house would go up in flames, imagining as I heard fire sirens that they were coming to our house because my mother had accidentally set us on fire. Even the fruit trees planted outside my window—by my father, who exulted in California's year-round good weather—became sinister. The nectarine, apricot, and orange trees that gifted me their fruit during the day became huge monsters on my bedroom wall at night whenever car headlamps shone on them. I would cry for my parents, but they only shushed me and told me to go to sleep, said that I had an overactive imagination, and that I was perfectly safe. These are the same people who told me the world was a dangerous place.

At four, when my adenoids were removed, I was taken to the hospital under the pretense that we were going over the canyon to my mother's sister Pearl's house. Instead, I was taken to a children's ward and held down by two nurses who pulled down my underpants and gave me an injection. I remember the glass syringe and terror. I woke up in a large white crib with metal bars to see my mother smiling at me from the other side of the room, eating Chinese take-out with a fork out of white boxes.

Apparently, tonsils serve as some kind of protection against psychic harm, according to the anthroposophists. So, adenoids out, hold the tonsils. Two days of Jell-O, ice cream, and Popsicles—which in truth wasn't so bad, because it was sugary, artificial, un-bioenergetic food that was forbidden in our house—then my father showed up, and we drove home as if nothing had happened. My grandparents were waiting at our house for me, and when my grandmother saw that I had trouble sitting down, she pulled my panties down in front of everyone and started exclaiming in Yiddish about the extravagant, parrot-colored bruise at the injection site on my exposed butt. "She'll be fine," my mother said in English. And it was not discussed again.

My mother threw herself into the world of Rudolf Steiner and helped to start one of the first Waldorf schools in the United States, Highland Hall. I began attending at the age of two. I still vividly recall hanging from my mother's neck, sobbing, as she dropped me off every morning. I was inconsolable as she left me in the care of other anthroposophy fanatics who were as far from nurturing as teachers can be, unless you count military education.

Over the seven years that I attended, I was verbally and physically brutalized. I spent countless hours, in half-hour increments, ashamed, with my nose pressed into the corner of the principal's office, my legs quivering and my hands tingling from the blood pooling in them. I was hit for dropping a copper rod in eurhythmy, a form of expressive movement that relates to the tones and rhythms of speech. We moved our hands to simulate sounds; the letter *m* was palms facing opposite directions, held upright about a foot in front of our faces, and moving back and forth in opposite directions. Rods were added to the exercises to develop precision in movement. At age seven, we were supposed to have the coordination to hold up a rod, a hand at either end, parallel to the floor behind our shoulders, let it go, and gracefully catch it with palms held up beside our hips as the rod rolled down our presumably straight backs. I failed because I was too slow, or because my spine was not straight, and was punished by the eurythmy teacher, Hans, with a stinging slap across my cheek.

On my first-grade report card, Mr. Theo Bergen, my class teacher (elementary teachers in Waldorf schools stay with their class from kindergarten until middle school), wrote in fountain pen, in his loopy German script, "Frisky, wisky, hippity hop, Julietta is like a little squirrel. Unfortunately, she is able to both work and talk to the other students at the same time, which is very distracting for those children without so much energy as Julietta."

In the third grade, Mr. Bergen—who per anthroposophic principles was supposed to be my loving mentor and spiritual guide—grabbed me by both my upper arms and slammed me down into my chair. I couldn't stand up after that, not for days, because Mr. Bergen had broken my coccyx. My mother was called to come pick me up at school, where she found me bent into an L-shape with purple fingerprint bruises on my arms. I can't remember my offense, just that Mr. Bergen swooped down on me like a hawk after prey.

It was then that my mother's maternal instincts kicked in with ferocious passion.

"You *physically assaulted* her? That's what they teach

teachers in Waldorf education? Are you kidding me? She's eight years old and you're a grown man! What kind of spiritual guidance is that?" I could hear her yelling at my teacher and at the school principal, Helen Howenstein, and they listened to my mother because she was one of the school's founders. I was never hit after that, and the bene-fits of my maltreatment that day were being taken home early, given a warm bath with eucalyptus leaves in it, and snuggling in bed with my mother as she read me *David Copperfield*, which I didn't understand but it didn't matter.

I relished the time my mother would spend alone with me, when she wasn't running around on errands for other people like her Waldorf friends, or my grandmother or my aunt Pearl. Sometimes we just drove back and forth over one of the canyons, obeying my father's wishes for absolute silence so that he could write. We would kill time so that my father had his goddamn peace, with me bobbling around on the scratchy, woven back seat smelling my mother's acrid cigarette smoke and trying not to vomit. It was our private time together. Sometimes we'd take baths together, and on occasion she would let me help with the cooking. But Betty cooking was more of a guerrilla affair that usually involved a pressure cooker and frequent hysteria as dinner exploded on the kitchen ceiling. Pea soup dripping down the walls was memorable, not only for my mother's laughter but because I didn't have to eat the dreaded stuff.

Anthroposophy wasn't just our weekday diet. On Sundays, my mother took me to the Christian Community Church, in a small house on a street in Downtown LA. The Reverend Verner Hegg christened me when I was six months old, with Xenia and Michael Chekhov present as my godparents and namesakes—my full name is Julietta Xenia Michelle Appleton—and we continued to go to church until I was nine years old. I stood with the other children during the entire, hour-long service, all of us staring at the white, cloth-draped altar full of gold candlesticks and flickering flames, our legs shaking in the hot, still air, wondering who would be the first to faint. Sometimes one of us really did. What I recall most from those Sundays, besides my father's absence, was the beautiful white, purple, and blue passionflowers, with their stripes and spikes and perfect geometry, glowing bright against their green leaves and spilling over the back fence into the yard of the house-church. It was there that we ran at the end of services in order to escape the adults and the stagnant air that felt like a hand cupped over our mouths and noses. We pushed through the side door in the kitchen, tumbling against each other, a pastel cloud of smocked dresses and Peter Pan collars.

It was clear that between my parents and grandparents and the anthroposophists, my body did not belong to me. I had no sense of its power until I was in my teens. And it wasn't until I had my own babies that I realized that children are people. Before that, I suppose I thought that one's identity just got inserted at some point, although I was never sure how. I don't remember thinking about it; I just assumed that all children were burdens, and I never knew at what point they stopped being thought of that way. My mother didn't live long enough to stop thinking of me that way, and my father never stopped thinking of me as that way, if he thought of me at all. So, I learned parenting without role models, which ultimately may have been a good thing.

3

FAIRFAX

Every time I look for memories of being loved, I think of my grandparents. I spent a lot of time at their house. The half-hour drive over Laurel Canyon from the Valley was a challenge because I usually got carsick, and my mother's cigarette smoke turned my stomach even more than the curves. But once I got there, I felt safe. When their door opened, I could smell a mixture of My Sin perfume, chicken soup, mothballs, and fresh challah.

My mother's parents, Joseph and Celia Rashkin, lived in Los Angeles near Fairfax Avenue. When she was younger, Grandma Celia had been pregnant eleven times and had had six abortions. She and my grandpa moved to LA in 1949 to be near their two daughters, my mother and my aunt Pearl. Two of their sons, Dave and Saul, stayed in New York with their families, and their son Jimmy lived in Florida.

My grandma would bathe me in her deep double-bowl kitchen sink made of white porcelain. As she washed me, she'd fuss over my *klayne fisseleh* (little feet), "just like your mother's." She hovered over me, making sure I was all right, worrying more about me, my mother said, than she did about her own children. She'd make me hot tea with milk and sugar and pour it into the saucer for me to slurp with a teaspoon. She let me sit on the back of her armchair and brush her long, gray hair while she watched *Days of Our Lives* and *Queen for a Day*. Her favorite show was wrestling. I separated her hair into two long ropes and twisted one around the other.

"Does the braid look pretty, Grandma?"

"Julietta, *mein* hair iss poifect," she'd say, even though we both knew it wasn't really a braid. "*Du bist a shayneleh.* Give a kiss."

Her cupboards always seemed empty because she made everything fresh daily, from scratch, even noodles. The only items she regularly kept stocked were Ritz crackers, yellow raisins, and 7UP. That was why my mother always shopped for her.

My mother also shopped for Aunt Pearl, who never left the house unless her husband was with her. She was married to a man named Alfred, a Viennese Jew. Uncle Alfred was the manager of Chasen's, the restaurant with chili so famous Elizabeth Taylor would have it sent to Rome while she was filming *Cleopatra*, and he brought food home every night for his family. Occasionally he cooked his specialty, sweet and sour string beans, but mostly they ate whatever was on the menu at the restaurant. If Aunt Pearl needed something from the market during the day, like some fresh cantaloupes, she'd call my mother and ask her to drive over Laurel Canyon into town and buy them for her. And if her neighbors offered to go shopping for her, Aunt Pearl would always say, "No, let Bessie get it. She's coming in anyway," even if she wasn't. My mother was always worried about her little sister, not only because she was afraid to leave her house but because she had threatened to kill herself several times, and my mother was afraid she'd really do it one time. Getting her cantaloupes was just an excuse to check up on her.

My grandpa was calm and steady to be around. When he was home during the day, and it wasn't Shabbos, he'd take me for walks. We'd stop at the toy store, and he'd let me buy a Barbie outfit each time. My favorite was gold lamé with a pretend mink collar. He also bought me whatever I wanted to eat, which gave my mother fits. Grandpa let me eat Jell-O powder right out of the box, with a little bone spoon. If my mother found out, she yelled at Grandpa in Yiddish. My grandparents just politely ignored her preferences, as they ignored her conversion to Christianity. I doubt they knew about my mother's unorthodox folk remedies.

One Friday night when I slept over at my grandparents, Grandpa took me with him to synagogue. I was eight years old. I'd never been to a synagogue before in my life. He and I walked holding hands in the soft darkness, listening to the crickets, and smelling the night air. We walked past the glow of streetlamps and down a street with neon signs, including one that said "Burlesque" and had a woman's shape outlined in pink neon with her leg kicking up and down from her knee. Grandpa kept his head down. When we got to the *schul*, he took me upstairs and sat me down alone in some seats overlooking an area below filled with more seats. There was a kind of table in the middle.

He went downstairs and joined several other men, and they swayed back and forth and chanted in Hebrew. It sounded strange to my ears. I was used to hearing English and Yiddish, which both my parents spoke at home. But only at my grandparents' house had I heard Hebrew, usually before meals or when they lit yahrzeit candles in memory of the dead. This night, after the men chanted, they held up a scroll, chanted and bowed, and put it away. Then they said Kaddish, the mourner's prayer, in Hebrew. Finally, they shook hands. Grandpa came up to get me then brought me outside to greet his friends. They shook my hand, or kissed my cheek, and said, "*Gut Shabbos, klayneleh.*" We walked back to his house, smiling and holding hands, and I felt that something special had taken place, only I didn't know what. I understood, without words, that we had been in a holy place.

The closest we ever came to having a party at my grandparents' house, besides Passover, was the night Kennedy got elected in November 1960. As far as I was concerned, it was better than a Passover seder, because on Passover there was always a fight between people in my family. It was usually about something stupid, like the texture of matzoh balls or who had a better job. Once, Uncle Jimmy got upset with something his sisters or parents said and stormed out of my grandparents' house from a seder to go back to the airport and book a return flight to Florida. I think someone insulted one of his shady Florida land deals. I liked Passover because I read "The Four Questions" and got to find the afikomen, the hidden matzoh, and get a prize for it. Usually a silver Liberty dollar coin. But the election was great fun.

All my LA relatives were there, and my mother's cousin Harriet was visiting from New York. She danced around the house with me in her arms, calling me "Miss Applesauce," and said, "Pow, right in the kisser!" as she planted kisses on my mouth. Everyone cheered the wins for Kennedy. We stayed up late, waiting for the final election tallies. I fell asleep in my mother's arms and woke up in my own room as my mother undressed me on the bed and put me in pajamas. The house felt joyful, and so was I.

4

SOLA

It was Monday, June 19, 1961, and I was nine years old. I walked into my house after being dropped off from school (my best friend Connie's mother usually drove us) and found my living room full of relatives I barely knew. In my bedroom, I discovered my Uncle Harry and Aunt Clara. Uncle Harry was a psychiatrist and a magician. I liked him because he could do card tricks and make things disappear, but I was always a little afraid of him. My parents treated his advice like words from God, and if he told them I should not be helped with my homework, for example, they listened to him and ignored my pleas for assistance. He had basset hound eyes and smelled like old pipe tobacco. I waited for him to do something amusing, but he was serious.

He sat me down on my bed and said he needed to talk to me. Aunt Clara, her eyes magnified through her black cat-eye glasses with little rhinestones in the corners, bent her head and began to concentrate hard on taking things out of my dresser and putting them in a suitcase. My suitcase, I realized. She folded my short-sleeved, floral cotton pajamas, some cotton panties, shorts, and my white sleeveless blouse with the ruffle across the chest and lay them carefully in the little gray valise that had stitching around the edge.

"Julietta, do you know why all these people are here?" my Uncle Harry asked.

"Yes," I said as I turned to look at him. "Because my mother is sick. She went to the hospital last week." I looked back at Aunt Clara, who was bending down in my open closet and reaching for my white Keds.

"Julietta, look at me," said Uncle Harry. "Your mother's gone."

Gone. Gone where?

"You mean she's dead?" I asked. Aunt Clara glanced up, looked away.

Gone. So simple.

"Yes. Why don't you help Aunt Clara pack some of your things? We'll drive you to Connie's to stay for a while. This is no place for a child."

This, I had thought, was my bedroom. I am a child. It *is* my place. My mother is dead, and you're taking me away from my house. If you can pull quarters out of my cars, why can't you bring my mother back?

My heart pounded, my tongue turned to sawdust, hot poison poured through my veins and seeped out onto my palms. My fingers were numb, my chest was being crushed, I needed someone to save me, but no words came out of my mouth. Uncle Harry left the room, unable to deal with my shock, and Aunt Clara sat down next to me on my bed. She patted my hand, then stroked my head.

Clara was my father's baby sister. She was fifty-five and

had no children, so I guessed she made up her own rules for how to act around kids. That was part of the reason I liked her so much. When I slept over at their apartment, she let me stay up late and eat food that my mother forbade in our house. We made brownies together, and I got to lick the bowl and the beaters. She cursed in front of me and was especially fond of shouting, "Shit, piss, and corruption five hundred times in the same place!" when something got her mad, like a run in her stockings. I thought she was, as my father put it, "one tough broad."

But now my aunt sat next to me, helpless. She had no idea what to do. I desperately wanted a grown-up's arms around me, my mother's. Even my father's. I heard his voice somewhere in the house, but he didn't come in. In a panicked stupor, I walked to the bathroom and got my toothbrush and tube of Pepsodent, then returned to my bedroom and picked up my stuffed monkey. I added them all to the valise. Not one word passed between me and Aunt Clara, who I could see was now crying silently, her chest muscles contracting rhythmically as tears slid down her cheeks. Uncle Harry came back to my room to get us, and they drove me to Connie's house. I have no recollection of walking past my other relatives on our way to the front door, but I remember that my father didn't say good-bye. And that the leaves of the camellia bush off our shaded front porch were cold as they brushed my legs when I walked past.

In retrospect, I wonder how someone like Uncle Harry, a psychiatrist, a doctor trained in the care of people's emotions, their deepest feelings of normalcy and stability and belonging, could have been so callous in telling me my mom had died. My sense now, as an adult, maybe misguided, is that psychiatry in the 1950s and 1960s keyed on keeping women and children in the dark. I think of the show *Mad Men*, where character Betty Draper lies on her psychiatrist's couch weekly and shares her heart, and then all the secrets she's entrusted him with are shared with her lord and master, Don Draper. Was Uncle Harry going off script in being honest with me? Was he really being callous or was he grieving too? Should he have told me something else? If so, what? I know kids are sometimes told their mom is in Heaven now, or with the angels, when she dies. Should Harry have told me that? Would it have given me more comfort to believe she was some *place* maybe I could get to, rather than asleep forever?

At Connie's, we were trying to make things normal again, as if by going about our usual routines we could rearrange life the way we arranged miniature cardboard Vic Damone albums in Barbie's Dreamhouse. We played a game about the future, using paper folded into triangles with our fortunes written inside. We held it over our thumbs and index fingers, open and close, open and close, like paper snapdragons. We found out who we'd marry, how many kids we'd each have, where we'd live, if we'd be rich.

We went swimming. Connie was teaching me to do somersaults underwater. I was terrified of being upside down, certain that I'd never complete the revolution and the sky would be stuck below me forever. Which was why I forced myself to do it, propelled myself past my fear and the agonizing shock of hearing about my mother's death, seeking comfort in the warm, enveloping pool that I hoped would erase reality. If I could spin backwards, maybe I could reverse time and bring her back, bring back my life as I knew it. Me, a mommy, and a daddy.

My head broke the surface and I gasped. I had done it. Somersaulted and survived. The chlorinated water stung inside my forehead. I somersaulted again, and again. But no matter how many times I turned, forwards or backwards, I still emerged into the same North Hollywood sun. The mica still glittered in the poolside cement where we were forbidden to run, the water droplets still evaporated into the same hot June air, and my mother was still dead.

Connie and I lay on towels afterwards, drawing water pictures on the cement. Her portable transistor radio, propped up by its little metal kickstand, played "Itsy Bitsy Teenie Weenie Yellow Polkadot Bikini." The tinny music shimmered in the air like a mirage. I was at her house for as long as it took for my father to "take care of arrangements." I'd never known anyone who had died before. I had no language for this. Connie didn't either, so we didn't talk about it. But it was there between us, the only thing that really was there. Everything else was like a flat postcard. The orange trees in the backyard, the blue sky, the hot summer day. I was so stunned I couldn't even cry.

Dinner seemed almost normal except for the bread, which Connie's mother and my mother had baked together a few days before, like they did every Wednesday. It occurred to me that this was the last loaf of bread my mother would ever make, and it stuck in my throat. I didn't want anyone to eat it, I wanted to keep it. Have my bread and eat it too. Now that expression made sense, but I knew the idea was ridiculous, impossible. No one talked about the bread, or about my mother either. This time no one teased me and reminded me that I used to say "small turd" cottage cheese instead of small curd. No one laughed loudly. In fact, hardly anyone spoke. I couldn't wait to leave the table.

After dinner Connie and I took a bath together and drew more water pictures, this time on each other's backs. First, she soaped my back up until the suds were thick, then took her finger and drew a letter, a number or words. It felt good. I didn't guess the letter right on purpose, so she'd have to draw more. Then, when I'd guess, it was my turn to draw. I drew single letters of the alphabet. Then words. Love. Mom. Soap. Shit. Fuck. By now we were rowdy and ordered out of the tub. If we'd been at my house, my father would have threatened us to be quiet by taking his belt off and wiggling it under the door, like a snake. It used to make Connie giggle, but I knew he meant it because my behind had been in contact with the end of that belt. Spankings at my house were often lashings, and I never could understand how hours after a transgression, like cracking the glass of the shower door with a shampoo bottle, a punishment could be meted out by my father with such dispassion when I had forgotten the incident and moved on. (Except for having to pay my mother for the shower door, with eighteen of my saved Liberty dollars.)

We watched a show on Connie's new color television. Sitting next to her, I felt the heat radiate from Connie through her thin pajamas. I felt sad that it wasn't my mother's warm body beside me. I thought about her growing cold somewhere, and I felt like ice had just been poured into my body. I shivered. Connie's mother told us it was time for bed and tucked us into separate bunk beds, with a kiss apiece. Her father came into the dark room and entertained us by making designs in the air with his lit cigarette.

His hand spun quickly, and the glowing tip became a circle, a squiggle, a square. Then he kissed us goodnight, whiskers and tobacco breath, and was gone from the room.

Connie fell asleep right away. I heard her parents talking quietly in their bedroom. Their television clicked off and then I heard them say my mother's name. I heard water running in a sink, a toilet flushing, and then the lights were turned out. In the complete darkness, I felt utterly alone. I wanted to run into her parents' room, I wanted to call my house, I wanted my father. I missed my mother. I lay stiff and frightened, my heart pounding. Hot tears ran out of my eyes and became cold on the pillow. I stuffed the edge of the sheet in my mouth so no one would hear me crying. I was ashamed that I was homesick. I wondered who would make the bread now.

The next day, I arrived at the chapel at Forest Lawn Cemetery with Connie's family. Everyone seemed to be dressed in dark, hot clothes even though the weather was warm and sunny. The sky was a vivid, crystalline blue. Shards of bright sunlight reflected off the cars parked in front of the chapel. I was dressed in a sleeveless, hot pink dress, with white horizontal stripes on the skirt. Attached to the dress in the middle of its white Peter Pan collar was a white fabric rose with green paper leaves. They itched my neck and poked me if I turned my head.

We entered the chapel doors and all eyes seemed to turn towards me. I heard murmuring. Up front was a shiny wooden casket, the color of maple syrup, surrounded by flowers. The lid was up. I felt sick. To the left of the casket, perpendicular to the rows of pews, was a padded pew full of my relatives. They looked like black-birds sitting on a telephone wire. Two aunts were wearing hats with veils. The only visible white was the collars and cuffs of men's shirts, glowing behind somber ties and jackets. An aunt motioned for me to sit with them. Where were my grandparents? My father did not even look at me. I felt a hand in the small of my back, Connie's mother, propelling me forward. But I leant back against it instead. I didn't want to sit with my family. It was bad enough that I was the dead woman's child; my pink dress would make me stand out like a Siamese fighting fish in a bowlful of mollies and everyone would stare at me more. And the coffin terrified me. I didn't want to be near it. Instead, I sidled into the last row with Connie's family.

A family friend, Bob, played classical music on a silver flute; there were speeches by my mother's friends and speeches by teachers from the Waldorf school. I tore up an entire boxful of tissues into a mound of soggy flakes. Around me people were sniffling and blowing their noses. Occasionally, I heard a loud sob.

Finally, Bob played another piece and, row by row, people moved forward to walk past my mother's coffin. Some stopped for longer than others. I had no idea what I should do. At least I'd be one of the last ones up there, but the eyes of my relatives would be on me. Finally, I arrived at the head of the coffin. My mother lay there, eyes shut, in a pale blue, wool bouclé suit. Her face was powdered and looked too orange, and her lips were painted a very dark red. Her hands were folded on her chest, and in one hand was a red rose, in full bloom. I had given it to her in the hospital four days earlier, picked out of our backyard garden when it was still a bud. I looked at my father, but he wasn't looking at me. He had his head buried in my aunt's neck. I could tell he was crying because his shoulders were shaking.

The first time I'd ever seen him cry was four days earlier, after we visited my mother in the hospital, before the second heart attack that killed her. When she had the first one, on a Thursday, she complained to Daddy of chest pains and he called her doctor, Dr. Knauer, the homeopath. He told my father to put sage compresses on her chest. When the pains didn't go away, my father drove her to Mount Sinai Hospital and had her admitted while I was at school. On Friday he took me to visit her. That's when I cut the rose to bring her. I wrapped the stem in a wet paper towel and tin foil.

In the hospital, she smiled weakly at me and introduced me to her roommate, an old lady with wispy hair that stuck out all over her head. "This is my daughter, Julietta. She's nine, and very smart." She stroked my hair. I wanted to grab her hand and pull her out of the room, into the car, and bring her home with us. I asked when she would come back. "Soon," she said. That was the last time I saw her alive.

Following our visit, Daddy and I drove home from the hospital over Laurel Canyon. My father was silent.

"Is she going to die, Daddy?" I asked.

He burst into tears. "I don't know. I don't know."

"I don't want her to die!" I cried.

"I...don't...either, Sugar," came out in wretched sobs.

"Daddy, I'm scared."

"So am I, Julietta. So am I."

Her second, fatal heart attack must have happened at the hospital soon after we arrived home. But my father kept it from me, through the weekend and long enough for me to go back to school, and for relatives to get on flights from the East Coast and get lifts to our house.

After her funeral, in the parking lot at Forest Lawn, Uncle Harry put my valise into the trunk of our Chevrolet Impala. Twentieth Century-Fox had even put a car phone in it for my father. Sometimes I called Aunt Pearl on the way to school, just to call from the car. Whenever we stopped for gas on Ventura Boulevard, the attendant always came out to greet my father.

"Good morning, Mr. Leonard. Fill'er up with ethyl?"

"Yes, please," we'd both say. I had no idea why gas was named after a woman, except maybe she invented it, like Louis Pasteur had milk named after him.

My father had a big office at Twentieth Century-Fox. He shared it with Anna Mae Hart, also in publicity, who had a dachshund named Heidi who Anna Mae brought with her to work. Gene Kelly had an office nearby, and I remember sometimes he'd come in to give Heidi a treat. Once, he shook my hand. At Christmas, I got to go with other studio employees' kids to meet Santa, who sat in a sleigh on a set covered with artificial snow as he handed out toys to us in the hot December sun.

Showing affection was not easy for my father, not like it was for my mother. He hardly hugged me or touched me. Sometimes I was allowed in my parents' bed with them on weekend mornings, to sit on top of the covers on my father's bent knees, and then he would straighten his legs really fast and drop me and I'd laugh. Once my mom asked him to take me in the shower with him, and it made me uncomfortable, his thick man-penis right in front of my face as he soaped himself and the suds ran through his pubic hair and down his hairy legs. He never did it again, and I was glad.

On the way home from the funeral, my uncle drove our car, and my father sat next to him. I sat in back between my father's two sisters. As we drove, I discovered why my mother's parents, my only living grandparents, were not at the funeral. Forest Lawn was not a Jewish cemetery, and my grandparents were Orthodox Jews. My mother was to be cremated, and I thought that, like me, they were angry that she was going to be burned; I didn't know it was against their religion.

My father told Uncle Harry that my grandmother offered him $5,000 not to have her cremated. "But I couldn't go against Betty's wishes," he said. Uncle Harry said if my mother didn't have a will, my father didn't have to do what she wanted. My father said he was tempted, not by my grandparents' meshuga Jewish beliefs against cremation, but by the money. Then he remembered I was in the car and the subject was changed.

There were lots of people back at my house. Relatives, friends, neighbors, and my grandparents. They squeezed me and kissed me, and my grandmother started crying. "Oy, oy, oy, *meine shayneh maydeleh*. What's going to be with you?" She looked terrible. She was thin, her long gray hair was pulled back very tight in a twist, and her cheekbones stuck out. That day, she looked more frail than usual. Her eyes were red and puffy. What I didn't know was that she had metastatic bone cancer and would be dead in six months.

"Oy, my Bessie is gone!" she wailed. She never called my mother by her English name. My grandfather, who was nine inches shorter than my six-foot tall grandmother, put his arm around her thin waist. His navy suit smelled like mothballs. The dark blue made his eyes seem even bluer. He was the only person in my whole family with blue eyes.

"Shhh, shhh, shhh," he told her. "You'll frighten the *kind*." He led her to a chair. Aunt Pearl brought my grandmother a cold drink and sat with her. My grandpa took my hand and led me out of the crowd, into our backyard. The fruit trees created a lush fantasyland that my parents and grandparents could only have dreamed about in their native Russia or living on the Lower East Side of New York City.

Grandpa and I sat next to a guava bush, and he took out a pocketknife. One by one, he picked me guavas and cut them in half. He was a tailor, and his work was exact. I sucked the sweet, rose-colored flesh out of each one. Soon, my pink and white striped lap was full of powdery, green-gray guava skins. Then we walked over to my father's compost heap, which was steaming in the sun. My grandfather dug a hole with the tip of his shiny black leather shoe. I leaned forward and dumped the guava shells into the hole. Grandpa used his foot to cover them up, then tamped down the rich black soil. He took my hand again, and with his eyes closed and head bent forward, he began to say Kaddish.

5

VILLACH

After my mother died, I was passed around like a library book, living with friends, at sleepaway camp, at boarding school, and at my house on Sarah Street. At first, I spent time at the Walds', in Topanga Canyon, where Mrs. Wald tried to follow in my mother's footsteps and give me a coffee enema but inserted it accidentally into my vagina with me screaming not to be touched. At night, I'd look at the moon outside my window and pretend my mother was there and pray to her.

Then came Camp Idyllwild, sleepaway camp for stars' kids. The morning the camp bus left, from the Du-par's parking lot at Farmer's Market, my father insisted I eat a bowl of oatmeal for breakfast. Normally I would have had blueberry pancakes with blueberry syrup, but that morning I had no desire to eat. He forced me to finish my oatmeal and walked me to the parking lot. I rushed to a low hedge and threw up, unable to keep food down because I was so anxious.

I cried, "Please don't make me go! I promise I'll behave! I won't disturb your writing! Please!" to no avail.

"You'll be fine, honey. And I'll be up to see you in two weeks on Parent's Day."

"I won't be fine. I want to stay with you. Please. I won't be any trouble. I don't want to go!"

My father steered me to the steps of the bus with his hand on my back and gave me a quick kiss on the cheek before he propelled me upward. There was no resisting, as a line of other children had formed behind me. I barely remember the ride, except for the fact that I was queasy the whole way and fearful of the unknown.

The air at Camp Idyllwild smelled of hot pine sap, the paths to the cabins were dusty, and the color wars in the last week did not enthuse me. I was still reeling from my mother's death. Tootsie Pops were a sad comfort on movie nights, held outdoors on a huge screen, with films like *The Blob* terrifying most of us nine-year-old girls. After Parent's Day, which made me want to go home even more, I remember the devastation I felt as my father got in his car for the ride home to Studio City without me, homesickness sucking at me like quicksand and tears streaming down my face. The counselor was all forced cheerfulness, telling me we'd have fun in the next two weeks, but I couldn't believe it.

After the summer of 1961, I spent fourth grade at the posh Chadwick School, a boarding school where Hollywood stars sent their kids to live. To get rid of them, more like it. At least that's how it felt. I cried a lot. The school had an enormous swimming pool and a swim team of high school boys, the outlines of their penises showing in their tight bathing suits in the photo in the school yearbook. My dorm of fourth-grade girls tried to make suds in the pool by emptying a whole box of Mr. Bubble in the shallow end and jumping up and down. We were unsuccessful; the water stayed smooth and blue and chlorinated.

Our dorm mother, Mrs. Reynolds, was very kind and loving. She put her hair in pin curls every night with bobby pins. The night *Carousel* was shown at Chadwick, our entire dorm of girls hid under their beds afterward, sobbing for lost parents, with distraught Mrs. Reynolds feeding us ice cream sandwiches at eleven o'clock at night to console us. My mother was dead. My best friend Debbie's mom had just committed suicide. We were not a happy group, and the romantic premise of *Carousel*, that a dead parent could come from Heaven and spend just one day with us, tempted us and gave us false hope. Or dashed our hopes because we weren't being visited by any of our dear departed.

My father showed up one weekend at Chadwick to take me out to lunch at the Pink Parasol. He casually mentioned as I was eating my club sandwich that my grandmother had died of cancer two months back. I was shocked and burst into tears.

"But I didn't get to say goodbye to her!" I cried.

"It was a small private funeral," my father insisted.

"Were Uncle Dave and Uncle Saul there like for Mommy's funeral?"

"I don't know," my father said.

"Why not?" I asked.

"I was not invited," he replied.

"But it was Mommy's mother!"

"Yes," he said, "but they consider me persona non grata."

"What does that mean?" I asked.

"Basically, that I am not welcome in their lives."

I pushed my sandwich away, my appetite gone. Another loss in my family. Who was next, I wondered? Would my life become my own version of *David Copperfield*? And why on earth had my mother chosen to read an eight-year-old *David Copperfield*?

Often control came in very small increments that mirrored my reduced world. I'd arrange stuffed toys on my pillow or set my books in rainbow order on the shelf, or refuse to eat fish, or hide candy to eat at night, alone, that sweet first hit on the tongue a blissful blanket of memory suppression. Eating a warehouse full of sugar would not stop the sere, vast emptiness created by the loss of my mother that I felt then and still do. Or maybe I don't miss my mother but the idea of what a mother should be. I cannot imagine having a mother now and doubt that we'd get along as adults. I've had to grasp control of anything in reach to keep myself upright and rooted. Is this the bane of the only child? Of the motherless child?

I lived at home for fifth grade and attended public school, where my father told me that if boys bullied me, I should knee them in the crotch, which they did and which I did. We had regular drop and cover drills to prepare us for nuclear attacks, but mostly, besides scaring us, they were opportunities for the boys to pinch our bottoms as we huddled, curled into balls, under our desks.

Outings to the supermarket with my father were a delight, as we bought anything our hearts desired and didn't have my mother, the food fascist, critiquing our purchases. The freezer filled with TV dinners and the fridge with sodas, and snacks included things like Bugles corn chips and Tang to drink. The only time grocery shopping became terrifying was during the Cuban Missile Crisis in 1962, when everything was wiped off the shelves and there was not milk or bread to be had, and I was certain based on television news reports that we would die from a nuclear attack because we didn't have a bunker. No drop and cover was going to save my ass, I was sure of it, and I was very frightened. Fortunately, those thirteen days in October passed without us being blown to kingdom come, and food returned to the supermarket shelves as life returned to normal.

By 1963, when I was eleven, my father had decided that we needed to leave the United States and move to Europe. His attempts to get me adopted by another family had fallen through. Pearl and Bill Sholl, close family friends with two teenage sons, had offered to adopt me, but it didn't work out for reasons still unknown to me. I often wonder how different my life would have been if I had stayed in an intact family in the San Fernando Valley and grew up like a "normal" child. I realize that no family is perfect, that pretty much every family is dysfunctional, that everyone is damaged in some way whether small or large. If I had grown up a Valley girl, would I have been as interesting, would I have mastered five languages, would I have been as independent, or as fearful, or as resilient, as I am? Doubtful. But I might not have had as severe a panic disorder triggered by practically anything that involves my losing control—elevators, airplanes, surgery, drugs, alcohol, sometimes even letting go to have orgasms.

My father had stopped working at Twentieth Century-Fox before my mother's death, perhaps due to the effects of McCarthyism, but I was too young to ever know the details. Now he had to stay home and take care of me. He was also working on finishing the manuscript for *To the Director and Playwright,* and I vividly remember looking at the book galleys with him. Since his only asset was our house, he knew we needed to live somewhere less expensive than Studio City. He advertised in various newspapers in Spain, Italy, Austria, and France: "American writer and 11-year-old daughter seeking room and board." The responses piled up, and my father chose Austria, presumably because he had memories of being there as a child named Chaim Apfelbaum, before escaping to the United States. He sold our house for $24,000 and we moved, taking with us just our suitcases. The artwork from the house was put in storage, the rest of our belongings sold or given away.

We flew to Copenhagen (via Greenland, to refuel, where I got a stuffed seal toy), my first ever plane trip. I clutched my seal and the stuffed toy turtle that Pearl Sholl had given me. The plane was filled with cigarette smoke and a leering drunk on the flight terrified me. In Copenhagen we spent several hours in a taxi touring the city and visiting a department store (where I got a blond-haired doll) before flying to Vienna. From Vienna, it was a nine-hour train ride to Kärnten, in southern Austria, where my father intended to interview a few families before deciding on where we'd settle. I became ill on the train and remember vomiting the whole way and my father having to pay a schilling for a cup of *wasser* and being outraged that they would charge him for water.

Spent, we arrived in Villach, Kärnten, and checked into a hotel. It was March and there was snow on the ground, a sight I'd not seen before. My father ran me a bath in the deepest tub I had ever been in, washed me with a telephone shower, dried me off, and tucked me into bed under an enormous duvet. The cool, smooth sheets with the cloud of comforter above me was bliss, and finally I was able to relax and sleep.

The family we moved in with, the Messerschmidts, seemed lovely at first. Tony Messerschmidt had a huge pot belly, and his wife Edith was dark haired with thick glasses that made her eyes look very far away. Their twenty-two-year-old daughter, Inge, lived there, too, with her frizzy red hair and an oily patina of tiny pimples on her face, as did Frau Messerschmidt's mother, an ancient woman who stayed in her room and watched television. There was also a cocker spaniel named Cici who peed on the floor every time she greeted me.

Their house was not yet finished. The downstairs had carpeting and furniture and was where Tony and Edith and the grandmother all slept; upstairs were bare cement floors and built-in closets, all of which echoed whenever my father or Inge or I walked around. The stairs were also bare cement, and my father became infuriated when I clomped down them in my red Dr. Scholl's wooden sandals as he was trying to write.

There was a telephone shower and a bidet, and once I discovered the pleasures the bidet could provide, I used it so much I caused a leak over the dining room table, one floor below. No one mentioned anything about the wet ring on the ceiling, or its cause, to me, and soon the bidet was fixed and the ceiling dried out. My aquatic pursuits must have been a source of amusement for the Messer-schmidts and my father, rather than a reason to get us kicked out. Undoubtedly, the Messerschmidts needed our rent money to complete the second floor, but we didn't stay long enough to see that happen.

Frau Messerschmidt made me strawberry frappés from the wild strawberries I picked in the woods, and I ate more kinds of wursts and breads than I knew existed. Her Wiener schnitzel was divine, and we all spent a lot of time going on picnics to the many lakes around us. I swam in all those lakes, even swam all the way across one and back, alone, to my father's chagrin. There were wild raspberries to be picked, but I didn't listen to warnings not to eat the pale pink ones and threw up more than once on our drives home. My father bought a car in Vienna, a robin's-egg blue Taunus (a West German Ford), and that bought us freedom to visit places without the Messerschmidts.

My father often went on trips without me to Venice, meeting up with fellow artists he found through "Letters to the Editor" in the *International Herald Tribune*. Word of mouth led him to discover where many of his McCarthy-traumatized compatriots were calling home now that Hollywood no longer signed their paychecks. The Messer-schmidts didn't seem to mind being left with me for an overnight or two, but my father probably paid them.

One place I went with my father was to an Austrian drive-in theater to see the American film *Giant*, starring James Dean, Liz Taylor, and Rock Hudson. It was dubbed. In retrospect, it's hilarious. Then, I was awestruck by these huge American heads gargling in dubbed German, though my German was not good enough to understand it all. My father used his proficiency in Yiddish to understand it, but likely he'd seen it already when it came out in 1956.

Given my father's Yiddish-accented German, the Messerschmidts must have guessed we were Jewish even if

I didn't know it. Perhaps they saw renting to us as some form of post-war atonement, although I am not sure how they knew we were Jewish before we got there. Then again, maybe the rent money sweetened their distaste.

I knew little about religion other than from church on Sundays and from my Waldorf education, and as far as Judaism was concerned, I assumed that only my grandparents were Jewish but not my parents. I had been instructed by my father that if anyone asked, we were freethinkers. It was all really beyond my mental grasp, and I have mostly fond memories of our time in Austria.

But my father's disgust was not tempered. One night, Tony stood in the open doorway of the outdoor patio, backlit by the surreal flashing of summer heat lightning, and peeled dry strips of sunburned skin off his prodigious belly, popped them into his mouth, and told my father about his and Edith's days in the Hitler Youth groups. There were no raised voices, and there may have been some laughter, but something in my father changed then.

"Julietta," he told me as he tucked me into bed, "tomorrow I want you to be very sneaky and pack all your things into your valise and leave it under your bed. Don't let anyone see you. Put your stuffed toys on your bed like you usually do so the room looks normal."

"But why?"

"Because," he said, "we are going to leave in the middle of the night, and I don't want the Messerschmidts to know we are going. Let them find out after we are gone."

"Did we do something bad? Are we in trouble?" That was always my first instinct.

"No, honey. More like the Messerschmidts did something wrong, a long time ago. I'll try to explain it to you as we are driving."

"Driving where? Where are we going?"

"We're moving to Italy to live near my friend Jim. I'm going to start a theater with him. I need you to go to sleep in your clothes and not make any noise when I wake you up. Our secret, okay?" He put a conspiratorial finger to his lips and I agreed.

My father once told me the story of interviewing Howard Hughes, who lay in bed during the entire conversation. At the end of their visit, Mr. Hughes jumped out of bed to say goodbye and he was fully dressed in a suit. I felt a little bit like Howard Hughes, only poorer, as I climbed into bed that night.

My father woke me in the deep dark. Everyone in the house was asleep. He carried my valise, and I carried the stuffed toys. We walked wordlessly past the rooms of Inge, Tony and Edith, and Grandma and Cici, and let ourselves out the front door. I got into the back seat of the Taunus, my father gently snapped the trunk closed, and together we rolled quietly out of the driveway, headed through the Dolomite Mountains to Italy.

6

ASOLO

By morning's light we'd arrived at the farm of Tittoto
Primo (his twin went by the surname of Tittoto Secondo)
in Asolo, Italy, in the Veneto region. It was summer and
gorgeous, with lion-colored earth and silver-green olive
trees, the houses glowing pink and white and golden
against the bright blue sky. My father's friend in Asolo was
Jim Moon, an American artist with whom he was going to
start a theater company in the castle of Caterina Cornaro,
last queen of Cypress. The vineyards stretched before me,
the cows lowed in the stable, there were persimmons to be
plucked off the tree, and my fears of abandonment
stopped clutching me quite as hard.

My father and I shared a small space off Tittoto
Primo's main house. We had a living room, a tiny open
kitchen, and a bedroom upstairs. We did not have a bathroom of our own and had to use a chamber pot at night so
as not to disturb the Tittotos while they slept. I did not
remember, until I went back to the Tittoto farm as a fifty-
year-old, that my father and I also shared a bed at the

farm. That is probably why he sent me to live at Santa Dorotea, a Catholic boarding school, so that I would have my own bed—albeit in a roomful of twenty other beds just like in the children's story book *Madeline*—and a proper bathroom. But that was not before I was hospitalized, twice.

The food in Italy was, and is, the best I have ever eaten. My father and I would get veal roast rolled around sprigs of rosemary, coarse salt, and pepper, and cook it in the little kitchen. Or we'd go into town, to the Albergo del Sole or the Hotel Villa Cipriani, and eat cream of vegetable soups, *salumi* and cheeses and olives, risottos with saffron, pastas with wild boar or ground meat a la Bolognese, and sweet zabaglione for dessert with espresso. Italy is where I learned that food was not a punishment or a treatment for illness but a celebration for the body and soul, something transcendent. I drank watered-down wine with my meals, tasted grappa with my coffee. Consumption of food was always accompanied by the tinkling of glass and chiming of knives and forks and the raucous communion of happy voices.

I had an Italian tutor, Giulio, a young man in his twenties, who drove me everywhere on the back of his red Vespa motorcycle and taught me to speak Italian while sitting on walls at the Cornaro castle or picnicking out in fields sharing bread and cheese. I'd climb on the back of the Vespa and put my arms around his waist. I had never held another person other than family this close before, with so much of my body touching theirs, and it was exhilarating. What made it even more so was the fact that I believed I was in mortal danger most of the time I rode with him. I couldn't get enough.

I grew daring about what I ate. The Tittoto farm was like an open-air market, and I sampled its wares. But I should have been more careful, and one day after eating a bellyful of wine grapes right off the vine, I woke up with knife pains in my gut. Since we didn't have a phone, my father woke the Tittotos and they called the doctor who drove to the house and examined me in our double bed. I could not bend my legs nor bear the doctor's hands pressing on my stomach. Gastritis, he pronounced, from eating grapes sprayed with arsenic, the insecticide that Tittoto Primo used in his vineyards.

I was driven to the hospital and given a private room. My father stayed with me. By the second day with no food, I was feeling better and beginning to get hungry. I asked the doctor, "*Cosa posso mangiare?*" *What can I eat?*

"*Mangi acqua,*" he replied. *Eat water*. Which I did for another two days before I was released home with instructions to eat only gentle, cooked foods.

The second time I was hospitalized in Asolo was for an appendectomy. Coming home from a dinner at the Hotel Villa Cipriani I started feeling ill and had a full-blown panic attack because of the way my body felt out of control. I sobbed and shouted at my father as he drove.

"I need a hypnotist to stop these thoughts! I'm scared! Make them stop!"

"Julietta, I need you to calm down."

"Daddy, I have been trying to tell you I don't feel well since we were eating dinner and you didn't pay any attention to me. Don't tell me to calm down. This is your fault. I wouldn't be so sick if you'd taken me home sooner. Please, please make these thoughts stop! I don't want to die."

"You're not going to die, honey. It's a stomachache. And we'll call the doctor as soon as we get home."

He drove us back to the farm and once again asked Tittoto Primo to call the *dottore*. This time it was appendicitis, and I was rushed from the house right into the operating room, screaming.

"*Mio padre, mio padre!*" I cried into a masked face.

"*Sì, sì, sì,*" the doctor lied. "*Dormi allora.*" *Sleep then.*

I woke up in the women's ward, which had beds in rows down either side of the large room. Women and girls were bandaged in various places on their bodies, one woman wrapped like a mummy from her gas stove blowing up. Once my ether wore off, I was allowed to eat. Every morning nuns in white habits would bring carts of steaming, sweet caffe latte in large bowls. They gave each of us a bowl, a fresh baked roll, and a spoon. We tore up the rolls into chunks and put them into the coffee, where they got soggy absorbing the liquid. Then we scooped the meal up with our spoons.

After I was released from the hospital, I was sent to the Santa Dorotea convent school for the rest of the summer, until public school started. There were only three other girls there with me, and our voices would echo in the cavernous room. The ceiling was two stories high, but it was hard to see during the day because the shades were drawn down against the heat and the room was dark except for the bands of light at the bottom of each tall window. At the end of the row on the far left was an enclosure about ten feet square made by four curtains hung from metal frames. I soon learned that the nun who chaperoned us at night slept on a bed behind those curtains.

Next to each bed was a little wood bureau. It reminded

me of the hospital. I was instructed to put all my belongings there. As I started to unpack, my fear of being alone in an unfamiliar place began to take hold, and I felt the push of my guts holding down my terror. With dry mouth and shaking legs I put my things away, wishing I could run away to my father but knowing I was too weak from my surgery to even try.

A nun stood and watched me organize my belongings. I had difficulty standing completely straight. My black stitches were still in and poked my underpants whenever I moved. After unpacking, the nun handed me a towel and led me to a bathroom. She started filling the tub for me and said she would be back to get me after my bath.

She closed the heavy door behind her and then I heard a key turn. I listened for her footsteps to recede, and then tried the door handle. She had locked me in. I felt the fear rise into my chest again and leaned against the cold wall to hold myself up. I needed help getting into the tub and help with washing and drying myself since the surgery, but I wouldn't have dared ask. I felt as if no one could hear me even if I shouted. My voice would just echo off the walls.

This bathroom was as bare as Aunt Clara's bathroom was plush, and just as big. I looked around, planning an escape route if I needed one, and saw there was no way out except the locked door. There was a window with no curtain, but it was up very high. The floor was gray-green marble with shiny flecks. The same color marble came halfway up the walls, and above the marble the stone walls and ceiling were painted white. The sink and tub were white. There was no toilet. The only thing on the wall was a rosewood crucifix. There were no towel racks, only a hook on the back of the door. I hoped the nun would come back for me.

I turned off the water. The faucet leaked. I had tremendous difficulty getting my clothes off. My stitches stuck out like plastic whiskers from three black knots. The scar was a raised purple welt about two inches long, low on the right side of my belly, and itchy. I held on to the edge of the tub, and slowly, painfully, lowered myself until I was sitting in the deep, hot water. It burned my incision, but it felt almost as good as scratching it. I realized with dismay that the bar of soap was up on the sink. I decided against getting out of the tub to get it, so I lay there and listened to the faucet drip. It echoed off the walls, the bathwater sounding like a deep well. I closed my eyes and wondered how much time I would have to bathe, what would happen to me if the nun came back before I was dressed, and how I would manage to get out of the tub on my own. The only softness in the room was the towel and my clothes; everything else seemed hard and cold. If this room were in a game of Animal, Vegetable, or Mineral, it would definitely be mineral. Even the water seemed somehow metallic, a transparent greenish broth whose surface fractured whenever the faucet discharged. I let my head slide down the back of the tub until my hair was underwater, only the oval of my face exposed. The water slid into my ears, but I could still hear the distant plop-pause-plop of the faucet. I hooked my toe under the brass chain that held the rubber plug and tugged it out. The water began to gurgle down the drain.

Somehow, I got myself out of the tub, dried myself, and got dressed. I combed my hair with my fingers. Then I sat on the edge of the tub and waited. Finally, *finally*, the nun returned and let me out. I went to lie on my bed until the other three girls arrived, but I felt lonelier with each new addition. They all knew each other from the previous year and spoke in rapid-fire Italian. I was a true rarity and they made sure to let me know it.

The girls chattered around me and peppered me with questions that I struggled to answer in my rudimentary Italian. They asked me questions about the United States, and Hollywood, and I asked them as best I could how to cope in Catholic boarding school. They thought this was funny since everyone is Catholic, no? You're not? What are you then? Oh, a Hebrew, *ebrea*. I still did not think of myself as Jewish. They couldn't define me, and I couldn't either.

Every evening around dusk, a bell sounded for vespers and several days later, when I had recovered enough to go with them, I followed the girls to chapel. We walked along gravel paths edged with neatly trimmed English boxwood hedges that smelled fruity in the sun. The chapel was scented with smoky perfume, and there were several nuns there, including the Mother Superior. Everyone murmured in Latin, and I just copied the movements of my roommates. Up, down, kneel, sit. Then we moved forward to kneel at the front of the chapel at a railing. They opened their mouths; I did the same. Suddenly the Mother Superior rushed up the aisle with her skirts and long crucifix swooshing, exclaiming in Italian, "No, no, NO! She hasn't had her First Communion!" At the same time, I felt her hand around my upper arm, and she pulled me to my feet and sat me back down in the pew. Humiliated and unholy, I sat and waited in shame for the girls to come back to the pew. Then we filed out to the dining hall in silence.

Everything was unfamiliar to me. There was an air of strictness and the threat of punishments to be earned, yet we could buy beer or chinotto soda with lunch and dinner, and after meals cabinet doors were thrown open in the study hall to reveal bins and bins of candies that we could buy so long as we didn't leave the wrappers on the floor. My favorites were the Jordan almonds and the sour fruit candies that came in cellophane and melted if you pressed them against the roof of your mouth with your tongue.

I never went to the chapel again. There didn't seem to be a point. And no one forced me to go. I remember the nuns walking around Santa Dorotea, rubbing their rosary beads between their fingers and shaking their heads about poor Signora Kennedy in Washington because she had lost her little baby Patrick. They prayed for her and told me so, as if as an American I had a direct connection to the White House.

One day after about three weeks of Santa Dorotea, my veins filled with anger at how the nuns and the girls poked fun at me, teased me because I didn't share their traditions, because I simply didn't fit in. I shouted at a nun and called her "*Pinguina!*" a word I'd heard my father say when we'd seen nuns walking in town. I knew it was an insult. The nun grabbed me by my ear and dragged me outside, where we faced each other standing on the gravel between the hedges, in brilliant sunshine. She slapped me hard across the face. I could feel my lip swelling.

"*Pinguina!*" I shouted again. "*Pazza!*" *Crazy*.

She raised her hand to hit me once more, but I turned and ran back to the dormitory. I packed all my things into my suitcase and marched to the main building. The

Mother Superior was waiting for me in the vestibule. Shaking with anger, I pushed past her.

"I'm calling my father." She didn't try to stop me.

Tittoto Primo's wife answered the phone, then ran to get my father. He picked up the receiver, breathless. "What's the matter?"

"I am not staying here!" I screamed. "How could you do this to me? They hit me! I don't belong here! I'm Jewish! And I'm not going to put up with this! I don't care what your friend Jim says about this place. I want to live with you. Either you come and get me or I'm walking back."

And I hung up.

I really didn't believe he'd come, and as I trudged down the gravel drive, I imagined him sending me back to the States alone, as he'd threatened to do so many times before. He'd tell me I was selfish and demanding and too much to take care of, that he was sending me back to live with someone who really wanted me and slam his door in my face.

So, I was calculating where I wanted to live and with whom I wanted to grow up when the turquoise Taunus pulled up.

My father turned off the car and got out. He put his arms around me and held me, and I buried my face against his shirt and cried. He didn't say a word to me, and when I was empty, I looked up at him and saw tears in his eyes too. He picked up my suitcase and put it into the back seat. We got into the car and drove into town, to Rino's Caffè Asolo. We both had cappuccinos and almond biscotti. My father read the *International Herald Tribune* and I worked behind the counter, washing cups and glasses for

Signor Rino who stroked my head affectionately and called me *cara mia*, "my dear one." My father never apologized, but within weeks he found us a new place to live that had two bedrooms, and at the end of the summer I started public school in Asolo.

7

TREVISO

We were installed in the attic on the third floor of a villa in Treviso, very close to Asolo, owned by a countess, which impressed me until I found out that one quarter of the town had titles like duke or duchess or countess or baron. It meant nothing really. The contessa obviously needed the income from boarders but couldn't even buy proper furniture. She furnished our former attic with a bridge table, two metal chairs, two single beds, and two dressers. We had two bedrooms, a bathroom, a central room, and a weensy kitchen. Our water was heated by a tiny propane tank whose blue flame I was certain would burn the whole house down. Or maybe the gas tank for the stove would blow up and burn my face and leave my hands bandaged like the young woman in the hospital ward.

It hardly mattered since we didn't spend too much time there. Once again, our lives settled into a routine. I went to school during the day, which was taught by nuns, but they were much nicer than the ones at Santa Dorotea. In the afternoons, we met at Rino's where I'd do my homework and my father would read the paper. We'd either go home and I'd cook for us, because my tutor, Giulio, had taught me to make pasta and sauces, or we'd eat at the Dante Due Mori. Some nights, my father would drive me home to get to bed and then go back to the restaurant.

One night he didn't return, and I was anxious. I tried to stay up all night, with the lights on, listening for the car on the gravel, but I kept dozing off. I worried that he had died somewhere and wondered how I would find out. Would the police know I was his daughter and where I lived to come and tell me? How would I get back to the States with no money? How could I access his bank account if I was just a child? My thoughts tormented me.

The floors were bare, unpolished wood the color of dust. I remembered the first night in the house on Sarah Street back in Los Angeles. I was alone in the dark, in a crib left casually by the movers out in the middle of the room. The floorboards were bare, the room echoed. I stood holding onto the crib bars, crying, screaming in the direction of the closed bedroom door, only a thin line of light visible at the bottom, my sliver of hope. I felt the tears and the mucus on my face, the hoarseness of my voice. No one ever came.

Finally, at seven thirty in the morning, I heard the Taunus pull up.

"Where were you? I thought something happened to you, that you might be dead!" My throat was tight with fear and anger, and my voice came out sounding like a whine.

"It's none of your goddamn business."

"I was worried!"

"My only obligation to you is to give you shelter, keep

you fed, and get you to school on time. And here I am, ready to take you to school. So, what's the problem?"

"Where were you?" I asked again.

"I stayed at the Dante Due Mori. Lina, the owner, arranged for me to have a room so I could write in peace. It's too noisy here."

I knew he was lying, that he'd stayed with Lina. Lina of the furry armpits who always flirted with my father when we ate there, who was impressed by the American writer. One night we ate there with my father's friend Jim, and my father had commented, "Seeing a woman with hairy armpits is like getting to see her sex with her clothes on," to which Jim, who was gay, replied, "I wouldn't know," and they both laughed. That was the Lina my father was talking about.

I was furious with my father for scaring me by leaving me alone all night. He knew I was afraid of having people I loved die, or of dying myself. Maybe the latter wasn't a rational fear, since I was only eleven, and my father tried to reassure me often. But I felt that living with a sixty-three-year-old father I might as well have been living with my grandfather, since he was older than all my friends' dads, and I lived with the worry that he would die soon. I got dressed and grabbed an apple to eat in the car on the way to school. I didn't speak to him, and when he dropped me off, I slammed the car door.

By now it was October, and the air was getting cooler. The windows steamed up inside Rino's, and when I walked the paths around school there were glossy brown chestnuts all over the ground. Sometimes things have their own unique smell, like boxwood bushes, or chocolate melting for brownies, or narcissus, but other things smell like something else that may be difficult to identify, at least right away. It would be several years before I could match the scent of chestnut trees with anything else. And then, I would know that their sharp pungency smelled just like semen.

In my father's quest for patrons for the Cornaro Theater, we took excursions to places outside Asolo, like Bologna, Bassano del Grappa, Florence, and Venice. Neither of us took my schooling very seriously, since I had learned most of the material already in the States, and I sensed that my father was getting anxious to move on if the Cornaro Theater project didn't work out.

We spent a whole week in Venice while my father tried to get a Guggenheim Fellowship. We saw the landmarks, traveled by gondola, and drank coffee in the piazzas. He ate lunch with Peggy Guggenheim while I stayed at the hotel. As usual, he came back empty handed. We went to Harry's Bar almost every night, staying until two or three in the morning. Our table always attracted American actors and actresses and directors and publicity people, all of whom my father knew. I tried to stay up as long as I could because everyone, everyone except my father anyway, treated me like a little pet. But I usually fell asleep on the banquette next to my father. Only Marilyn Monroe would have kept me awake, and she was dead.

I had never forgiven my father for promising to have her at my eighth birthday party when he knew she couldn't come. She called me during the party and apologized but it wasn't the same. I wanted to see my friends' faces when she showed up with her arms full of presents because she knew my father, and because my godfather, my Papa Misha, was her acting teacher. My mother was still alive then, and she got angry with my father for getting my hopes up. My grandparents had just laughed at me when I said Marilyn Monroe was coming to my birthday party. They didn't believe me or have faith in anything my father planned.

On the nights my father didn't take me with him to Harry's Bar, he left me alone in the hotel room. I was eleven. I got used to sleeping there alone at night with all the lights on and imagined that my father was right down the hall, even if he wasn't. I reminded myself that he was usually home to take me to breakfast, and I stopped questioning my father because now I knew he was with some woman or other, probably one of the cotton candy-haired actresses who'd swigged peach bellinis at our table earlier. He was vain about his looks, and he was handsome even in his sixties. He could tell charming stories and had an almost British accent, which was really a modified version of the English he learned on the Lower East Side. It was how he pronounced things that somehow fooled people. Or maybe it was his arrogance, but he sounded posh somehow.

Back in Asolo, my father continued reading "Letters to the Editor" in the *International Herald Tribune* every day to locate former film-industry people now living abroad who might be able to help him out. He had developed bursitis in his right shoulder, and it ached more and more as the weather grew colder. He'd sit at Rino's and massage it, or order anisette with his coffee, and Signor Rino would wipe the counter with a damp rag and recite, *"Dopo quarantina, dolori ogni mattina." After forty, pains every morning.* Like my father, Rino was in his sixties. They'd nod their heads at each other, wistful for days lived with more fire.

My father discovered that an old Hollywood colleague,

John Allen, was living on the island of Ibiza. Also a screen-writer, John and his wife had a house in Santa Eulalia and he urged us to move to the warmer climate. He wrote us and said it was a great place to write, and there was plenty of nightlife. Lots of expatriates. By November we had loaded up the Taunus, said our goodbyes, and were on our way through Italy, Monaco, France, and Spain to get to Barcelona, where we'd take an overnight boat to Ibiza.

8

IBIZA

En route to Barcelona, we stopped in Arles, where we looked for Van Gogh's famous bridge, but it had been destroyed in World War II. We ate at an auberge—broiled tomatoes stuffed with breadcrumbs—lots of garlic, cheese, and herbs, and kept driving. We tried to decipher road signs, like one that looked like two black, rounded breasts rising against a yellow background. That one turned out to mean a dip in the road between two small hills, which we discovered as we sped through it and dropped like a roller coaster car. I shrieked with glee, and my father drove even faster through the next ones. In Barcelona, we ate *pintxos* in our hotel the night before we took the boat to Ibiza. I read Ernest Hemingway's *A Moveable Feast* on the trip because my father said Hemingway and his friend F. Scott Fitzgerald were authors who had been where we were. But the Hemingway book was vignettes about Paris between 1921 and 1926, and my father and I had not been there, and none of the names, like Gertrude Stein, were known to me. My curiosity was piqued by a scene in which

Hemingway examines Fitzgerald's penis in a public restroom (because Zelda Fitzgerald had claimed it was too small), and Hemingway concludes it's of average size. How did he know? Was he just comparing with his own or had he seen many others? There was not much for me and my dad to discuss because I knew nothing of Paris and next to nothing about penises.

I had no idea what my father was searching for exactly that was going to be helpful to him, but somehow, I felt like his accomplice. In Ibiza, we moved into an apartment in a town called Figueretas. The apartment had tile floors, and we could hear conversations through the walls and foot-steps and chairs scraping above us. It was temporary until we could find a house. The apartment was too noisy for a writer, but there were other Americans and foreigners living there, so it was always interesting. My father didn't even bother to enroll me in school.

I had started to grow breasts and pubic hair, the former drawing my father's attention and warnings: "Don't trust boys or men. They only want one thing from you."

He didn't explain what that one thing was, but he repeated his warning often. He also didn't seem too worried regarding my whereabouts so long as I was home in the evenings. On random evenings he'd demand, irked, "Where were you? I was about to call the police!" but those evenings were no different than any others.

Days I wandered around our neighborhood or went to swim at the beach, evenings I came home to eat with my father or feed myself if he were out. I wasn't fearful. I just felt increasingly independent if a bit lost and alone. I was eleven years old. At the beach I'd found a hole in some rocks, and through it was a small, enclosed ocean pool. It was about twenty feet in diameter and the pale blue water was about seven feet deep, with large rocks all around and a window of sky above it. On the bottom of the pool was clean white sand. The only way in was to climb down through the hole. I'd hide in there and float on my back in the water, letting the waves rock and soothe me. I wished I had a friend to share this marvel with, someone like Connie.

Ibiza in the early sixties was a place where many people came to hide. From the law, from their former spouses, from their lives. Every gathering reeked of pot smoke, and sangria full of thick orange slices sloshed in everyone's glasses. We spent evenings at Elaine's La Tierra, a bar owned by a woman from Brooklyn. There were baskets of sunflower seeds on every one of the low tables, and people spit the shells on the floor. It was covered with a thick blanket of them. Sometimes we went to Arne's Bar, in the Old Town. I loved Arne because he was sweet to me and because he spoke to me in Danish-accented English and because there were hundreds of empty birdcages hanging from his ceiling, all with the doors open. He said it was to remind people that birds should be free. He made chocolate mousse with pineapple chunks on the bottom and danced with me while my father sat with his friends.

I returned to the apartment one day and the cleaning lady was talking to my father in Spanish. I could understand enough of it because it was similar to Italian.

"*El presidente Kennedy fue asesinado. En* Dallas." She held her thumb up and pointed her index finger, like a gun, and held it to her temple.

"What is she saying, Julietta? John Dulles shot Kennedy?"

"No Daddy, she says President Kennedy was assassinated in Dallas."

"*Sí. Sí. Eso es.*"

"Oh my God." My father sank into a chair.

I went to make us some tea with milk and sugar. We sat at the table and drank it together in shocked silence for what seemed like hours. This was the president whose election had brought so much joy to my family. And now he was dead. Gone.

That night, the Americans in the area got together in our apartment to get drunk. John Allen was there with his wife. John's nose was always red, and his eyes were bloodshot, and he didn't shave enough. He was an alcoholic with gray stubble and sour breath. I liked his dog, Estrella, but I avoided him. Drunks frightened me. They grabbed for me and made remarks I didn't understand, but I knew they were sexual. I heard my father's warnings in my head. People from our building were there, and some Americans who were visiting the island. The noise was unbearable. I stayed in my room with Estrella, on my bed, with the door closed, but the sweet smell of marijuana seeped in, and I could hear glasses breaking and thuds of bodies colliding against the walls in drunken embraces. My door was opened by our neighbor, Albert, who had often leered at me or made remarks about how I was growing into a woman. Now he had his arm around a woman and was kissing her neck. They were both drunk and looking for a bed. I glared at him. "Go to your own apartment. Leave me alone."

The next week we found a house. It was on a little street in Figueretas with houses up and down both sides, no more than two blocks long. At the far end was a food store.

Our house was at the beginning of the first block, the second from the corner, and like all the others it was white-washed with a red tile roof and had almond trees in the small yard. My father had to go out each morning to prime the pump so we would have running water from the cistern. To bathe, we had to heat water on the stove, pour it into a bucket, and stand in the bucket in the bathroom. We'd lather up and rinse off as quickly as we could since the thick limestone walls of the house made it very damp and chilly. If it was really cold, my father would build a fire, and we'd put the bucket in front of the fireplace. Even though he would go to his room when I bathed, or I to my room when it was his turn, I always washed fast because I felt so exposed. I didn't want my father to see me naked, and I didn't want to see him naked. I felt certain this was a boundary I did not want crossed.

Our neighbor on the corner was an English widow named Alice. She had a clothesline stretched across her yard, and her lace brassieres fluttered in the breeze, sema-phores to my father's susceptible nature. Soon he was spending late nights in town with Alice and sometimes sleeping over at her house.

We spent weekends and the Christmas holidays at the Allens' house in Santa Eulalia. John cut down a small pine tree from his property and we decorated it. We put popcorn underneath to look like snow. By New Year's Eve, Estrella had eaten it all. On New Year's Day, we sat on the Allens' patio overlooking the ocean, John and his wife, my father, Alice, me, and the Johnsons, another expatriate family from Hollywood, who also lived in Santa Eulalia.

Grady Johnson had worked with Paul at United Artists and, like my father, was a writer in his sixties with a career forever changed by McCarthyism. He was nearly forty years older than his wife, Didi, and they had two blond children. Julie was five; Robert was two and still in diapers.

We ate paella that John's housekeeper had made, full of chicken and chorizo and seafood and fresh peas, the rice bright yellow with saffron, served in a huge shallow black pan with handles. Small lizards scampered all over the patio, and some even came right up to Grady when he softly whistled to them. He gave them bits of seafood. The low pine trees blew gently in the breeze and the air smelled of salt. As usual, neighbors drifted by, had a drink or two and left, and the day was indistinguishable from nearly all the others on Ibiza.

Didi and Grady had a white MG convertible. Didi would come into town from Santa Eulalia to go shopping and pick me up to go with her. I had acquired Spanish in practically no time, and I was a useful translator. Didi would talk to me about anything: what it was like to be pregnant and give birth, to be married to someone much older than herself, how different life was here from in the States. Didi was the first person I could really talk to since I had moved to Europe. It was Didi who told me the name for the pleasure I gave myself nearly every night, and that there was nothing wrong with it, except a lot of Catholics thought there was. She and Grady were about as Irish Catholic as they come, she said, but she believed in birth control, another thing that she had to explain to me. I felt like a child when I was around her, simply because she was a mother. Yet there were only fourteen years between us, and in the five months together on Ibiza, we formed a bond. I told her everything, and it was like having a girl-friend again.

John and my father seemed to have had a falling out, or maybe it was that my father was disappointed that John had become an alcoholic since his Hollywood days. Or that John was friends with another writer who lived nearby in Ibiza and whose wife invariably opened the door with a black eye or bruises on her cheek. It was scandalous to my father, but apparently de rigueur to John. I remember over-hearing their argument about it, my father insisting that he did not want to go over to that writer's home anymore. At least when my father drank he could still carry on a conversation, and he didn't beat anyone up.

As Didi and I grew closer, so did Grady and my father. When you are an expatriate, the smallest things can bind you, like being from the same town. You may have never spoken to each other when you lived in the same place, but when you find each other abroad, it's as if you've found family. To this day, my family is whoever the outsiders are, the expats, sometimes in their own countries. My father and Grady were both writers from Hollywood, both the same age, and neither considered the other to be a drunk. That was enough for them. Soon we were spending time with the Johnsons rather than with John and his wife. At night we'd sit outside on the Johnsons' patio, and Grady and I would play guitar and sing. Grady often sang "Cool Water," a song I didn't know but loved to hear him sing. We could see satellites making their way across the night sky, twinkling gently, moving so slowly you almost thought they were stars. But they floated by in baby steps and even-tually disappeared. I played chords and hummed harmonies to Grady's Irish ballads. Julie would go limp as a Dali watch in Didi's lap and fall asleep.

I had a few friends of my own, all blond and blue eyed,

not one Ibizan girl. I have a photo of my twelfth birthday party, which my father had for me at Arne's Bar, and at only five feet tall I towered over all my younger friends. We ate chocolate mousse and listened to The Beatles on Arne's jukebox and danced with each other. The bird cages swayed above us. It was during the day, so he didn't have any customers besides us. My father gave me a gold heart locket. Aunt Clara had sent me a box of hand-me-down clothes from the States, with my first pair of black kitten heels. I'm wearing them in the photograph, with one of the used dresses, and a black velvet bow in my hair. It's hard to tell if I'm smiling or squinting.

Narcissus bloomed all over the island, and the almond trees flowered. Peasant women wearing straw hats and long black skirts picked the fragrant narcissus, and they were on tables everywhere. At the post office where we got our mail, in the bodegas, at the store, in our houses. The air smelled wonderful, green and lemony from the narcissus and bakery sweet from the almendros.

Alice came over to cook for us but her food was awful. She made tomato aspic, and my father told me I was rude for not trying it. It was looked like Jell-O, jiggly and flat in the serving bowl. It had been flavored with tomato juice. I began to feel nauseated and knew I could not eat; this was disgusting in a different way than some of my mother's food. My father was angry with me, I could see that, and I was just as angry with him for assuming that I would let this usurper force me to do something I didn't want to do. I cooked for myself or for me and my father; I did not need another woman in our life.

I was an icy little bitch to Alice. I could see she wanted to move in on us and take over *my* household, or so it felt to me. She tried to charm me, but it didn't work. I wanted nothing to do with her. She wasn't my mother, and my father and I got along just fine without her, thank you. I may have been only twelve, but I felt adult-like in some ways because I had been left alone so often. My father could not have me be a child when it suited him and then leave me in charge at other times.

Alice and my dad went out a lot and came back with stories about crazy poets and artists who danced on table-tops at Elaine's or got drunk and threw plates and threat-ened to beat the shit out of anyone just before they keeled over onto the floor. I think Alice must have mentioned marriage to my father because he began to see her less and slept in his own bed more often.

I heard my father come home very late one night. I was lying awake in the dark, the sheets damp from the sea air, fearful and afraid to close my eyes, sure that thoughts of dying would take over my mind and I'd panic. The week before, I had read an article in *LIFE* magazine at the John-sons' house that said that when you are asleep, it is like being dead. That exacerbated my fears of darkness and of dying. I prayed for the sun to come up soon, since I wasn't frightened in daylight. But it was the middle of the night and day was far off. I got out of bed and went to my father's room. He stank of alcohol.

"You smell. How much did you have to drink?" I asked.

"You know me, Julietta. I can't drink much. It makes me sick to my stomach. I only had a few drinks." I tried to believe him.

"Can I sleep with you? I'm scared. I keep thinking about Mommy. And dying."

"Sure." He moved over to let me in.

I lay awake next to him, knowing I'd be safe now that he was home. I closed my eyes.

"Julietta?"

"What?"

"I think it's time you learned the facts of life." I felt instantly embarrassed.

"I think I know them, Daddy. Don't worry."

"Do you know how a man is built?" Oh God, I thought. I was so embarrassed by his question.

"Yes, Daddy."

He reached under the covers and took my hand. He placed it inside his pajama bottoms, on top of his limp penis. I was frozen.

"Don't ever let a man put this," and he pushed my hand against himself for emphasis, then took his hand off mine, reached inside my pajama bottoms and squeezed my vulva in his hand, saying, "here."

I pulled my hand back in shock and jumped out of his bed. My world was careening around me. I ran back into my room and slammed my door. I wedged my chair under the doorknob. I climbed into my own bed and pulled the clammy sheets over my head and lay there listening to the sounds of my racing breath and thundering heart. Even through the sheets I could smell the cloying scent of narcissus. They filled every air molecule in my room. I never slept in my father's bed again. I don't think I even hugged him after that. I couldn't bear to touch him.

The next morning, my father primed the pump and came into the kitchen to make tea, acting as if nothing had happened. Perhaps he didn't even remember. I was trying to open a box of oatmeal with a serrated knife. I was nervous, and the knife slipped and cut my left index finger above the knuckle. The cut was so deep I could see white inside. I taped it tight, and finally the bleeding stopped. It took weeks to close. I still have the scar, even though it's faint, a thin white indent in my finger. It's only because it's there that I know that night really happened. Otherwise, I couldn't trust myself to believe it.

9

CANARIES

Didi came by and picked me up in the MG, and I didn't tell her anything about what my father had done to me. I was ashamed, and afraid she'd yell at me for being in my father's bed. Or betray my confidence and yell at my father. So I didn't talk about it.

"Where are we going? This doesn't look like the usual way into town."

"It's not. I'm taking us on a little sightseeing trip to the salt flats. I figure we better hit all the tourist spots before we move."

"You're moving?" I felt the bottom drop out of my stomach.

"We all are. Didn't your father tell you? No, of course not. He treats you like you're not there. Both of our families are moving to the Canary Islands. We've rented houses right next door to each other. Isn't that exciting?"

My mind was trying to grasp all the information and put it in the appropriate places. We were moving, again. I was surprised and angry at my father for keeping it secret.

I shouldn't really have been since he kept everything else from me. Didi and Grady and Julie and Robert as neighbors. I liked that. Canary Islands?

"Where are the Canary Islands?"

"Off the west coast of Africa. But they belong to Spain, so you can still speak Spanish. You'll be going to the International School in Santa Brígida, where they teach in English."

"Do they have a lot of canaries?"

"No, it's from the Latin for dog, *canis*. Dogs used to pull carts there years and years ago. But they do have a whistling language there, I hear."

"And why are we doing this? What's wrong with Ibiza?"

"Too expensive, too many tourists. Grady and your dad are going to write. Maybe they'll get rich and famous."

"Yeah, sure." We both laughed.

I couldn't concentrate on the salt flats, although it was interesting to see the shallow, rectangular reservoirs of sea water and men spreading the drying piles of salt with big wooden rakes. All I could think about was how frightened I was to start over and what relief I felt that Didi and her family would be with me.

Within the next two weeks we had packed up all our belongings into boxes and were ready to sail to Las Palmas, the capital of Gran Canaria. The MG and the Taunus were lifted off the dock onto the ship and all our boxes hoisted into cargo nets and unloaded on the deck, where they were secured with the other freight. Four days later, Didi and I got into the MG, with Julie and Robert in the back seat, and followed my father and Grady in the Taunus to La Garita.

La Garita was a community of new homes, a Dutch-Indonesian neighborhood. No more pumping water from a well. We had running hot and cold water, big refrigerators, and gas stoves. Each house had high walls in front and on the sides, separating it from the street and the house next door, and each house was built around a small, central tiled courtyard that every room opened onto. All the houses had ocean views. We would sit at our dining room table and watch ships pass on their way to Morocco and elsewhere. The houses were landscaped with cacti and succulents and plants with bright red, yellow, and green leaves. Palm trees were planted here and there, and geraniums bloomed in almost every color. Since our boxes were not being delivered until the next day, Didi and I, the two cooks, agreed we had nothing to prepare food with and wanted to eat at a restaurant that night. Grady and my father said they had a culinary surprise for us.

Five blocks from our houses was an Indonesian restaurant, and that night I ate rijsttafel for the first time, an array of grilled meats and rice served with what seemed like a hundred condiments: toasted coconut, ground peanuts, cooked egg, shrimp chips called *krupuk*, chopped cucumber, sweet things, salty things, sauces, spices. It was heavenly, even to baby Robert.

Soon we were settled in, and I started school. I was nervous to have to start all over, yet again. But at least this time I'd be in seventh grade, the right grade for my age, and I'd be speaking English with my fellow students. There were two classrooms at the International School, the big kids and the little kids. I was in the group of big kids, seventh grade and up. Altogether there were about twenty students in the whole school. We had two classrooms in an old finca and had use of the library, the courtyard where we held plays, and the tennis court where we exercised. Each classroom had two enormous mahogany tables that we used as desks, our chairs set up all around the tables like we were at a Passover seder.

Our teachers were two Americans, Bill and John, who lived on the top floor of the finca and who were obviously a couple. Bill had an elegant grace and dressed casually in chinos and plaid shirts. He had very kind blue eyes. John had a dark pompadour and wore black Ray Ban sunglasses whenever he went outside. He always looked dapper and had the same kind of vanity my father did. When they weren't teaching, John painted pictures of still lifes that mostly had seaweed and driftwood and nets in them, and Bill cooked and kept house.

The fact that Bill and John were a couple didn't seem to matter to the principal, Mrs. Walston, a holy roller from Alabama who, it was rumored, was in love with John and followed him to the Canaries. Mrs. Walston's' first name was Bernice. Her gray hair was styled into a cross between a beehive and a bun, and heavily sprayed until it was stiff. She lived alone in a little house not far from the school where she read her Bible, listened to Andy Williams records, cooked grits and divinity fudge, and invited us over if she ever caught us behaving, which was rare.

One of the rudest and funniest girls at school was another American, Reny Slay, whom I fell in love with instantly. It was mutual. She was what I imagined someone who had been raised among wolf pups would be like. Wild, affectionate, playful, and sly. Her waist-length blond hair was a swarm of curls, and she often pulled her hair off her face with a huge, ludicrous-looking chiffon scarf tied in a bow almost the size of her head. Her blue eyes were usually opened wide so you could almost see the whites on top, and full of mischief. It was Reny who explained some finer points of sex to me and told me the difference between penises that were circumcised versus uncircumcised. I already knew about vulvas and vaginas from my mother, who was adamant about the difference between the two, and I learned about the rest from Didi. I also realized the fifth-grade movie on periods that I had seen back in the States was basically useless. It was Reny who taught me the real deal.

Reny was always plotting ways to frighten Bill, whose reaction when he was startled was so cliché and outrageous that it thrilled us and made us giggle. First, he'd put both hands up and shriek loudly, then clasp his chest, right hand over his heart, and then he'd smack the back of his right hand against his forehead as he closed his eyes and exhaled.

Reny once sneaked into our classroom early one morning and lay on top of one of the tables, eyes shut and hair fanned out around her like a shroud, with her hands crossed over her chest. I hid behind the door. When Bill came in to open the wooden shutters to let light into the classroom, he saw her and screamed and went into his gasping and clasping ritual. Mrs. Walston came running and had to break out the smelling salts she kept in her purse. Reny just sat up on the table and blinked, smiling an angelic smile. There wasn't much they could do to her since her parents were the school's primary benefactors. I stayed hidden because I had no trump card.

In biology, we learned about the reproductive systems of plants and animals. Each one of us had to give a report, and Reny rigged it so that I, who would do anything she put me up to, got the reproductive system of the male mammal. She convinced me to do a human and helped me with large, elaborate, colored drawings of a penis and testicles, full frontal and side angle, complete with pubic hair, which Reny thought was an authentic touch. When my turn came to stand in front of the class, poor Bill gasped and had to lean against the wall. Everyone in the class howled with laughter as I tried to keep a straight face and explain seminiferous tubules and the corpora cavernosa and the prostate gland, but I didn't get very far into it before Mrs. Walston showed up and ripped my two posters to confetti while she muttered about obscenities and vulgarities. Then she told us not to move or breathe or blink while she escorted Bill outside for a gulp of fresh air.

I loved nothing more than to go home with Reny after school and lie on her bed while we tickled each other's backs and listened to The Beatles on her record player. She showed me the best places to hide in the hills behind her house, where we sometimes sat in the sun with our shirts off and ate cactus pears. I was often invited to dinner and to sleep over at Reny's. Her parents were both painters, and their house had a black living room. Their paintings looked as if they had been done by wildly imaginative and talented children and were hung practically floor-to-ceiling against the black walls. Sitting on the living room sofa was like sitting in a garden painted by Henri Rousseau. I felt happy there and slept over at Reny's house as much as I could.

My father, with his usual lack of planning, had not calculated on the nearly ninety-minute round trip drive between La Garita and Santa Brígida. He got visibly annoyed every morning that he had to interrupt his writing and drive me to school. In the evenings, he was irritable. I always made us dinner when I came home from school, and the long drive pushed dinner back longer than he liked. I tried to talk to him about school during dinner, but he was often mean and moody. When he heard about my biology report, he was angry. I told him that Reny's parents thought it was funny.

"Well, I'm not Reny's parents, am I? They don't put a roof over your head or put food in your belly or buy your clothes, do they, you little ingrate!"

"You don't buy my clothes," I muttered. "Aunt Clara sends me hand-me-downs."

"Don't you dare talk back to me!" my father shouted and waved his knife at me for emphasis.

"I'm not talking back! It's true! You don't buy me anything! I wish you had died, not Mommy."

"I've had it with you," he yelled, and threw the knife at me from across the table. I ducked and it clanged on the tile floor. His chair scraped the floor as he pushed it away from the table and stood up. "Find someone else to live with. I don't care where. Go back to the States for all I care, if someone wants you."

"Please, Daddy," I cried, "don't do this! I didn't mean it! I'm sorry." But he went into his room anyway and closed the door. Later that night, he slid a list of names and addresses and several aerogrammes under my door with instructions to write all these people and ask if they'd take me in.

I was terrified that he would send me away. The list included Pearl and Bill Sholl and Aunt Clara and Uncle Harry. I imagined living with the Sholls and their teenage sons and decided that being with them, if they would have me, would be preferable to living with my childless aunt and uncle, despite Aunt Clara's warmth. Harry was cold and critical, and I would never forgive him for telling me my mother was dead. How would I tell the Sholls or anyone else that my father didn't want me anymore? Was I a bad kid? Did I do something terrible? Maybe nobody else would want me either. I was deeply ashamed. He didn't speak to me or come out of his room while I was home for four days.

It was not my father's death I feared, but his leaving me to fend for myself in getting back to the States and living without him. His crazy was known crazy to me; new crazy might be too hard to handle.

I went next door to Didi's, and she made me breakfast, took me to school, and picked me up at the end of the day for the rest of the week. By the weekend, my father had opened his door and come out, and he came over to the Johnsons' for dinner acting as if nothing out of the ordinary had happened and treating me like he always did, with a sense of amusement combined with annoyance.

My father decided that it would be easier for him if I lived at school during the week and came home on the weekends. I was mortified because he told me I'd be living with Mrs. Walston. But it turned out to be okay. I had grits for breakfast every morning, I learned to like Andy Williams, and I got to take flamenco guitar lessons twice a week. Although we didn't have an ocean view out our window like in La Garita, there was a beautiful poppy meadow instead of a backyard and a view of mountains. And there was Daphne, another girl I met at the International School.

Daphne lived near the school with her parents and two sisters. They were from North Carolina and had syrupy Southern accents, just beautiful. But Daphne was as fluent in Spanish as I was, and we spoke in Spanish so the American adults didn't know what we were talking about. Daphne often slept over at Mrs. Walston's and shared my bed. We practiced French kissing and read the sex scenes from *Lady Chatterley's Lover* out loud, like when Mellors makes love to Connie on the forest floor and she finally has an orgasm. In looking back, D.H. Lawrence can only imagine women being passive in order to enjoy sex, and he is quite conservative in his writing, even though at the time his book seemed risqué and graphic. It was not graphic. He describes thighs as "glimpsey" and breasts as "meaningful," whatever that means.

Daphne and I merely stroked ourselves, or each other, nothing that led to us having orgasms, but we each knew how to do that alone. With Daphne it was the first time I had agency over my body with another person and could allow someone to touch me and give me pleasure, not pain. I'd had so many assaults to my body—enemas, whippings, slaps, inappropriate touch, surgery, stitches—that sex and giving *permission* to be touched felt extremely empowering. I was the authority over my own body.

Mrs. Walston had no idea that there were budding sapphists in the next room, or if she did, she didn't care. One morning she teased me for having fallen asleep with *Lady Chatterley's Lover* open on my chest above the covers and made sure John and Bill were in on the humor too. They found it uproarious that a thirteen-year-old would be reading that, but no one censored me. My father always said boys only wanted one thing, but what he didn't tell me (or even know, maybe) was that girls wanted that one thing too, and Daphne and I found it. We were driven by our thirteen-year-old libidos, and it was wonderful.

On the weekends in La Garita, I spent a lot of time at the beach, and my Spanish friends showed me how to be adventurous. There were cliffs about thirty feet out from the beach that jutted into the bay, and they showed me the path to get up to them. The cliffs weren't that high, but when I was standing on the top of them looking down, I wanted to turn around and run back down the path to the beach. My friend Josefa just grabbed my hand and we jumped off together, landing in the soft, easy waves. It was a nice swim back to shore, being lifted by the water. We jumped off the cliffs over and over.

Like California, the Canary Islands didn't have seasons. The weather was almost always warm, even at Christmas, which I celebrated at Reny's. It was the first year my father and I didn't have a tree. Reny came home with me for New Year's, and my father took us to a concert in Las Palmas to hear the Israeli violinist Ivry Gitlis. My ability to sit through, and appreciate, classical music had improved dramatically since my mother had taken me years before. We sat in box seats in the ornately carved concert hall, the chandelier sparkling before the lights dimmed, and then I was mesmerized by the music. Tears dripped down my face as each movement reached deeply inside me, the violin singing with aching clarity and the orchestra supporting it. I didn't know that much beauty and passion existed. Reny kept handing me tissues and teased me afterward for being such a weenie. But I felt as if I had just learned to understand another language, and I couldn't explain that then. Thirty years later, when Reny found me again, and told me Bill was teaching in Japan and Mrs. Walston had moved to Greece, we went to hear the Philharmonia Virtuosi together in Peekskill, New York. We sat in the front row and held hands and let the music speak for three lost decades.

When school let out, I went to the beach every day. My skin turned brown, and my curly hair turned auburn. I learned the different colors of the ocean and how soothing it felt to swim in calm, high tide. I was able to tell the different kinds of boats that passed in the distance and got excited when I saw a clipper ship. I learned to avoid the big purple bubbles along the tide line, the Portuguese man o' wars with wicked strings that left welts wherever they touched your skin. I ate fried potato and bacalao patties and *sopa de lenteja* with my Spanish friends at the little bodega on the beach. The wife of the bodega owner did all the cooking. At night, we'd make bonfires on the beach and sit in the cool damp sand and talk. Sometimes I'd bring my guitar and we'd sing.

"Cuando calienta el sol aqui en la playa
Siento tu cuerpo vibrar cerca de mi..."

Every few weeks, little flannel cloths would appear on the clothesline strung up on the patio in the back of the bodega. Finally, I asked Josefa what they were for. She was astounded that I didn't know.

"Don't you get your period yet?" she asked in Spanish.

"No, not yet." I was thirteen. Reny had hers. Josefa had hers. Josefa's twenty-one-year-old sister had three kids. I was still waiting for my period. "Is that what they're for?"

"Yes, *boba*, what did you think they were?"

"I have no idea. But isn't she embarrassed to have them out there where everyone sees them?"

"No, everyone knows women have a *regla* once a month. What's the big deal? Besides, the sun bleaches them much whiter than if you dried them inside."

"Oh," I said, and was thankful that Reny had bought me a box of tampons, which was hidden in my underwear drawer.

That summer, I also learned to flirt with boys. There were lots of them in our little beach group, including Mateo, who was also thirteen. He made me blush and feel shy whenever I saw him, but powerful that I could have the same effect on him. The girls teased me, and Mateo responded by acting as if he didn't care about me at all. But one day as I lay on the beach, I felt something cool and slippery on my back. Mateo was tickling me with a dead octopus. I screamed and ran down the beach to get away from him. He chased after me grinning, his white teeth glowing against his brown skin, and his straight black hair flying off his forehead as he ran. The octopus dangled at the end of a stick. I ran into the surf, and Mateo still followed. I knocked the stick out of his hand into the water, where it and the octopus floated away.

Mateo yelled, "Hey, I was going to take that home and eat it!"

Nearly all the Spaniards at the beach lived elsewhere during the other seasons, but in the summer, they had little shacks made of plywood that they stayed in. The walls inside were lined with newspapers, which was replaced each summer. No bathroom, no running water, no kitchens, only portable gas stoves with two burners. It was more like camping. By comparison, my house was a mansion.

Mateo invited me to his parents' cabana. His mother

had made a huge lunch of lentil soup with potatoes and saffron, blood sausage and salad, with bread and guava paste, and *café con leche* for dessert. After lunch, during siesta, his mother taught me to crochet. In three hours, I mastered it. From then on, I brought my crocheting cotton and tiny crochet needle to the beach and made doilies the way Mateo's mother had shown me.

I made an effort to be at my house as much as I could to take care of the chores. On market days, twice a week, my father and I drove into town, where I haggled to get the best prices on produce and meats. I made sure that there were meals cooked for him in the refrigerator and that our maid, Antonia, had all the supplies she needed for cleaning. I could cook the basics—roast chicken, meatloaf, a beef roast that soaked in vodka and coffee for two days to soften the bad cut of meat that it was—and learned some Spanish specialties from my friends' moms, like lentil soup (you have to put the saffron on the pot lid and get it hot and dry before you crumble it into the soup) and arroz con pollo. I tried my best to cook with *gofio*, a roasted Canarian grain that, no matter how I cooked it (hot cereal, for example), tasted like burnt sawdust, so we nixed further experiments with it. Didi gave me a recipe for chocolate cake that had rinsed sauerkraut in it, which made the cake moist and tasted like coconut when the cake was cooked. Still, it was a weird recipe.

One night after I'd stayed up late cooking for the week, I crawled into my bed exhausted. I woke up in the middle of the night feeling something wet and sticky between my legs. I turned on the light and reached into my underwear. My fingers came out covered with blood. There was a wet red stain underneath me on the sheet. I got up and went to my dresser to get out my tampons. Thirteen and a half and finally I had gotten my period.

I took off my pajama pants and underpants and was standing with one foot on the floor, one foot raised on my bed, about to insert my very first tampon. There was a knock at my door.

"DON'T come in!" I said.

"Julietta, what's going on in there? Why is your light on at three in the morning? Who's in there with you? Let me in at once!"

I rushed over to the door and put my foot against it. My father pushed the door against my foot, and I wasn't strong enough to resist. He forced the door open while I pushed hard against it, using my hands now and leaving bloody fingerprints. He stood in the doorway, and I backed away from him into the center of my room, naked from the waist down, exposed, bleeding, humiliated.

"Get out. Now. I mean it," I said.

My father just stared at me, looking at the bed, my bloodstained hands, my naked pubic hair. A half-smile came to his lips.

"So, you're a woman now. Is this your first time?"

"It's none of your business." I reached behind me to the corner of my room and grabbed my guitar by the neck with my sticky fingers. I raised it over my head.

"I'm not kidding, Charlie. Get out of my room NOW or I swear I will crack this goddamn guitar over your head."

My father's face registered shock. I had never cursed at him before. I had never threatened him before. I had never called him Charlie before. It was the first time I had asserted my independence, and I was feeling violently protective of myself. I meant what I said, and he knew it. I was sick of his lack of trust in me and his suspicions that I would be as promiscuous as he was. I was done being treated as an irresponsible child. Maybe I wasn't a real woman now, but I was sure on my way. I would certainly have smashed my guitar to splinters over his head if he had continued to stare at me. But he moved awkwardly out of the doorway, fumbled for the doorknob, and closed my door. From then on, he left me alone.

10

PIETÀ

The new school year began. I now attended the Spanish public school, staffed by nuns. I wore a scratchy, black wool uniform, with a white short-sleeved cotton shirt underneath. Our housekeeper, Antonia, had to iron it to keep it crisp or the nuns would complain and mock me, which exaggerated my shame at being motherless. What I remember about the school was an open courtyard so typical of Spanish architecture, dark wooden shutters opened wide to let the air into the large, tall windows of the classroom, tiled floors and whitewashed walls, and long benches and tabletops instead of chairs and desks. And mean teachers. Fortunately, I only attended for about three months before our fate changed.

I lived with my father and his new girlfriend, a Dutch woman in her seventies named Katy. I liked her. She had her own bedroom and slept at our house maybe two nights a week. The rest of the time she slept at her own house. I was still in charge of the meals at ours.

We got a letter from Aunt Clara and Uncle Harry that

they would be traveling to Europe for two months before moving into a retirement community in Laguna Beach, California. They wanted to spend Thanksgiving with us, along with the friends they were traveling with. It was my responsibility to make the meal for us all. We managed to find a turkey and sweet potatoes and ingredients for salad, plus I found some lime Jell-O at the American supermarket in Las Palmas to make for dessert. I didn't know how to make apple pie even if we could have located all the ingredients. I was embarrassed that Aunt Clara, who was a wonderful cook, would be eating food that I had made. And it was not going to be traditional, no cranberries or stuffing or gravy, because of unavailability or my inexperience.

I had mixed feelings about seeing Uncle Harry again, but I loved Aunt Clara, and I knew she would be a kind reviewer of my food even if it was terrible. I managed to pull off the Thanksgiving dinner, even if I was a little embarrassed about the lime Jell-O. To even find Jell-O in the Canary Islands was quite a feat. Katy, my father, my aunt, my uncle, their two friends, and I enjoyed the meal on a sunny Thursday in November no different from other sunny days in the Canaries. In that respect, it was very much like California.

The meal was deemed a success, and I felt proud of myself for having pulled it off. But I could tell that my aunt and uncle were shocked that I was doing the cooking for me and my father, although they spoke in hushed tones about it.

My father and Katy spent a night in Las Palmas with my aunt and uncle, leaving me at home while they went to a nightclub, and, in retrospect, I wonder what Uncle Harry and Aunt Clara thought about my being left at home alone. Perhaps they just assumed that I had a babysitter. But I would have complained if I'd had one at that point because I'd been independent for so long. Didi drove me to school in the morning and by the time school was out, my father picked me up, and my aunt and uncle had left for the rest of their tour. I didn't long to return to the States; instead, I felt like a young Canarian who was on her way to meeting a young man and getting married, like Josefa's sister had at thirteen. I planned to wait four more years until I was seventeen, but I shared none of this with my father.

Soon Katy moved back to Holland, and my father and I were alone again. One Saturday market day, I waited for my father to finish his shower and shave. I sat by the front door on a bench, filing my nails and listening to my father's opera records. Once, weeks before, out of boredom and because my father loved the aria, I played "Che gelida manina" from *La Bohème* over and over and over, until I knew it by heart. I can still sing it to this day. As my father shaved, I hummed along to the record. Then I realized that I had been hearing the buzzing from the electric razor for a very long time. I was afraid to disturb my father, but I also knew that the market hours were nearing a close. I knocked, but all I heard was the sound of the electric shaver. Then, I heard a faint scratching against the bathroom door.

"Daddy?" I called with alarm.

There was no answer.

"Daddy!" I cried again.

I heard the scratching on the other side of the door. I tried to turn the doorknob. It was locked.

Now I was worried, and I ran for Antonia, who was in the kitchen.

"My father is not answering me, and I am sure there is something really wrong," I told her in Spanish.

Antonia ran to the bathroom with me and tried to open the door.

"*Señor!*" she cried out, "*Señor!*" to no avail.

We discussed trying to break in through a window, but there was no actual window in the bathroom, just a high transom. Breaking it would have showered glass onto my father and I was too small, even if Antonia lifted me up, to get over it.

Antonia ran to the kitchen and found a screwdriver. Somehow, with me crying hysterically at her elbow, she managed to unlock the bathroom door. My father, naked, his skin an ashen gray, lay slumped against the tiled wall of the bathroom next to the bathroom door, drool coming out of his mouth. He tried to speak but couldn't. Antonia picked him up, carrying him like the pictures I had seen of the Pietà, my father limp in her arms as she placed him gently on his bed. She covered him with a blanket and told me to go get the doctor.

Since we did not have phones, I ran to Didi's house, and she drove me to the *farmacia* in town. Dr. Noble was the brother of the pharmacist. I was embarrassed to see Dr. Noble again, because the last time had been when I had had a yeast infection for over six months, too ashamed to tell anyone. I had scratched myself raw with a boar bristle brush, and it was only after Reny told me about "galloping crotch rot" and urged me to go to the doctor that I finally told Didi, who took me. I was prescribed sitz baths and a cream to apply topically. God forbid a thirteen-year-old girl should insert anything up her virginal vagina, even if I did use tampons. And there was no way I was explaining that to Dr. Noble!

I now told Dr. Noble that my father had fainted, since that was the only word I knew in Spanish to describe his collapsing like that, and that he had to come immediately. Dr. Noble followed us in his car to La Garita, and when we arrived, we all went running in to see how my father was. Antonia had stayed by his bedside, and his color had returned somewhat, but he looked old and frail. He was sixty-five years old, and I thought that was ancient. I also was afraid I was about to become orphaned.

The doctor listened to my father's heart and breathing and checked his blood pressure. He asked my father if he had any pain. My father shook his head and said a slurred, "No."

"He's fine," said Dr. Noble. "He just fainted. He needs to rest a few days and eat nourishing food to get his strength back."

"But why is he talking like that?" I asked

"Doesn't he normally sound like that?" asked Dr. Noble.

"No," I said. "He sounds like he's drunk."

Dr. Noble asked my father to squeeze his hand with each of his hands, and it was at that point that the doctor realized that my father's whole left side was weak.

"He's had an *embolio*," said the doctor. "*Un ataque cerebral.*"

I had to look it up in the Spanish dictionary. A stroke.

I knew that was scary and could be deadly. Now I was certain I'd be losing my father, too.

Dr. Noble told me to get my father a rubber ball to

squeeze with his left hand, to regain strength on that side. He didn't tell him to go to the hospital or to see a specialist. I didn't know he was supposed to. The doctor left, Didi went home, Antonia went to heat my father up some soup, and the following week I bought my father a little red rubber ball.

11

LEAVING LAS PALMAS

Surprisingly, my father recovered completely. He must have had a TIA, a transient ischemic attack, or mini stroke, but at the time, that's not what we thought it was. And my father felt certain that we needed to return to the States. I didn't realize until three years later, when I was sixteen, that it was at that point in his life that my father decided that he could (or would) no longer take care of me, and that was one of the reasons we were going back. I just assumed he wanted to be around better medical care.

My father did not really communicate with me, just began making arrangements to return to the US, and my lack of trust persisted. I didn't know if I'd live with him when we returned, or if he'd hand me off to someone else. And would the someone else understand that I had been basically independent for years now, that I was used to my autonomy and would not respond well to being tamed?

We spent Christmas and New Year's Eve uneventfully. My father and I toasted each other with champagne at midnight on the eve of 1966, and he prepared me for our trip home via freighter from Scotland, which we'd get to via ship from Las Palmas to London, a train to Edinburgh, then train to Grangemouth, Scotland, and finally a freighter to Los Angeles. The freighter trip, through the Panama Canal, would take twenty-two days.

On January 5, we drove to the port in Las Palmas to see the Three Kings arrive by ship for their annual portrayal of the magi arriving to greet baby Jesus during *Dia de los Reyes*. Never mind that Jesus was born in a desert and it's highly unlikely that the magi arrived by boat. Three men dressed in long robes with long gray beards sailed into port to much applause from the small children and adults watching. Candy was tossed into the crowd, and there were dancers and puppeteers in parades through the streets of Las Palmas. The *horchaterias* were open, serving sweet horchata—pureed sugar, almonds, ice, milk, and cinnamon. My father and I sat with the Johnsons outside an *horchateria*, at a white metal table with chairs that had their white metal backs twisted into heart shapes. We compared this parade to the parades of *Semana Santa*, Holy Week.

Holy Week, the last week of Lent just before Easter, is celebrated with parades too, but it's a somber affair. Priests swing censers filled with frankincense and myrrh, crowds fill the streets to see statues of saints held up high on the shoulders of churchgoers and local politicians. Entire streets in Las Palmas are blocked off to cars and the road-ways are filled with a carpet of flowers in all kinds of colors and designs, often Moorish in nature. Only pedes-trians can pass, on the sidewalks. Despite the seriousness of the priests and the religious brotherhoods performing penance as they walk in the parades, *Semana Santa* could also be unruly. Drunken sailors roamed the Las Palmas streets, there were the occasional puddles of vomit, and it was the first place I saw nude male graffiti—erect penises and balls with whiskery pubic hair around them drawn in ballpoint pen on white calla lily flowers.

Dia de los Reyes was simpler but more festive. It's really a children's holiday and more popular among children than Papa Noël. It's when Spanish children get their holiday presents and often dress in costumes themselves, like the three kings. Streets are garlanded with lights and Christmas decorations. It was definitely more fun for me than the lot at Twentieth Century-Fox, even though I had outgrown Christmas. After *Dia de los Reyes*, we left the Canaries.

My father and I and our blue Taunus boarded the cruise ship in Las Palmas, after a tearful farewell to the Johnsons. I'd never been on a cruise ship before, and I don't know if my father had either. It certainly was nothing like the ship that brought him in steerage from Europe to the United States in his childhood. Every night on the cruise ship was a celebration, with party hats and confetti and a big band, white tablecloths and fine china and silverware. Couples danced and got drunk and cheered and clapped. We dressed for dinner every night as if we were going to a ball. I wore satin or silk hand-me-downs from Aunt Clara and my father his tuxedo, the one he used to wear to the Academy Awards every year before McCarthyism put an end to his Academy membership.

Once in London, my father took me to Harrods for high tea in the tea salon, and he bought me a gray and black checked wool coat and a black wool hat to protect me from the cold. These were the first new clothes anyone had bought for me in three years. We toured a bit of London by taxi. For dinner, we ate at Bentley's Oyster Bar, but I wouldn't touch an oyster then if you'd poured money directly into my veins. The following day, we boarded a train for the five-and-a-half-hour trip to Edinburgh. I spent much of the trip with my face pressed against the window, marveling at the countryside and the gentle snowflakes which fell on grazing sheep. I also played gin rummy with my father, a game he had taught me when I was eleven, the no-knocking version. We drank tea with milk and sugar at our seats on the train and finally made it to Edinburgh amidst a true snowstorm, my first ever.

I remember almost nothing of our time in Edinburgh or of the short train ride to Grangemouth or even of us boarding the ship. The freighter was most definitely not a party ship. There were only three passenger cabins, a total of six passengers, and the rest of the ship was staffed by officers and crew. The ship itself was painted white, the passenger lounge covered in an ugly brown carpet with beige floral patterns on it. There was a large dining table and eight chairs where we ate our meals every day with the captain, bookshelves filled with books, a greenish sofa, and some comfortable armchairs for reading. I spent a lot of time on the main deck behind a lifeboat, strumming my guitar, sunbathing, or else in the passenger lounge. I read, or tried to read, some of the library books but they were too old or boring for me. Instead, I discovered teenage sailors. Or specifically one teenage British sailor named Michael.

I don't know what my father thought I was doing on the freighter, or if he cared. Perhaps he figured that we were in effect stuck in a prison in the middle of the ocean and where could I go, after all? I remember seeing him very little. He may have been in our cabin writing, or in the lounge writing or reading. Or playing solitaire. But I heard none of his admonishments about boys and men only wanting one thing, as if he had forgotten. Yet here I was surrounded by young men. Enveloped. Sailors' heads turned when I walked by in my two-piece bathing suit. Sandy, the second mate, always scooped me up in his arms and hugged me when he saw me, and I was impressed by his bright white uniform and long bright teeth. I felt mighty having this kind of effect on men. I caught the eye of Michael, an adorable eighteen-year-old sailor who had curly dark hair and blue eyes, and I fell in lust.

Soon I was spending afternoons in Michael's cabin, up in his bunk. We French kissed, and we touched every part of each other's bodies. We didn't have intercourse, but we did everything else. I loved having his finger inside me, and his was the first erect penis I'd ever felt, the curly thickness of his pubic hair exciting me to wetness. I learned how to hold a penis in my mouth and suck it rhythmically, and I learned what semen smelled like. I refused to taste it though. Michael taught me that Brits called semen spunk, so when an American says someone is "spunky" I always laugh to myself. I learned the pleasure of cunnilingus, although I never had any orgasms with Michael. Part of my fear of losing control, I think. The Beatles always played on his record player when we were exploring each other, and "Ticket to Ride" held special meaning and sent us into giggles. How mature we thought we were. I got a feeling that Sandy, the second mate, wanted me too, but he was in his twenties and too old for me. I was mad for Michael. Our affair lasted the whole trip. I may have been rounding the corner of fourteen, but I was still only thirteen years old.

We reached the Panama Canal, where there are three locks at each end. The ships are raised as each lock fills with water, until they reach Gatun Lake, then the ships are lowered again. The trip from ocean to ocean takes eight to ten hours. We went from the Atlantic side to the Pacific side, stopping for a few hours in Panama City where my dad and I disembarked and went for a Coke. Panama City reminded me of the Canary Islands, with palm trees and banana trees and people speaking Spanish everywhere.

Michael had told me that I'd see dolphins and flying fish when we got to the Pacific Ocean, and although I didn't see dolphins, I saw fish zipping through the air making silver lines like Connie's father's cigarette squiggles. But aside from the Canal, all there was to see was ocean and more ocean. I spent as much time as I could in Michael's cabin when he was not on duty. It was hot and sweaty and sexy.

12

STATESIDE

Finally, after more than three weeks at sea, we reached the Port of Los Angeles. We were met by Aunt Pearl and Uncle Alfred. Aunt Pearl, to her credit, did not reach down into my pants and try to grab my butt cheeks in her usual greeting, so I felt more control over my own body. But she did exclaim, "Oh my God, Julietta! You look like a spic!" I had no idea what that meant, had never heard the word before, but I knew it was bad and to Aunt Pearl meant "other" in some way. I felt like I never belonged in Europe. I was always the Jew in a sea of Christians, even though I had not really been raised Jewish, and now I was back with family and I still didn't belong.

I soon realized that I was to drive home with Pearl and Alfred, and my father was going to live at Aunt Clara's. I was shocked and dismayed but not surprised because of my father's habit of sending me away. And he reassured me that he was only six blocks from me, so I could walk over and visit.

Pearl and Alfred's house was tastefully decorated but it

was sterile, as if the interior were left over from some photo shoot from *Sunset* magazine. There was no sign of human life, just furniture and attractive bedspreads. Everything matched or was color-coordinated. The master bathroom had a thick carpet, which made it feel like the softest and swankiest room in the house. The kitchen had nothing on the counters but the radio, which my fifteen-year-old cousin, Janis, and I listened to every night as we dried the dinner dishes and put them away. My favorite song was Stevie Wonder's "Signed, Sealed, Delivered."

I attended eighth grade at John Burroughs Junior High School where my cousin was in ninth. I knew she was embarrassed by me and neither she nor her friends had much to do with me. Aunt Pearl took me shopping at May Company for some new, American clothes, including a two-piece bathing suit that was navy on the bottom and ruffled yellow gingham on the top. She also took me to get my "spic hair" tamed. The stylist said I had enough curly hair for two people. Janis got the nape of her neck shaved into a W, like the wings of Batman, also a popular television show, but my hair was too curly to do that. Ahhhh, TV. I hadn't seen it in three years and basked in the fantasy life it offered me. *Star Trek*, *Mission: Impossible*, *Batman*, *That Girl*, *The Wild Wild West*, and Saturday morning cartoons. Aunt Pearl pointed out that my mother had been the theatrical agent for *The Wild Wild West*'s Ross Martin, who played the beloved character Artemus Gordon.

I was teased a lot at school. This was not new to me, but it felt crueler somehow that I had come back to America and yet Americans didn't accept me either. In my

English class, Mike Magnus thought he was hilarious by calling me "*Chuleta*" which means chop, like pork chop, and soon lots of kids started calling me that. I made my own friends, the other "outsider" kids who were Black or nerds or both. My best friend was Teri Jackson. Her father had died of syphilis, part of the Tuskegee Study, the first time I had ever heard of it. Black men infected with syphilis were left untreated to study its effects, and he had died of "syphilitic insanity," or tertiary syphilis. I was horrified. I slept over at Teri's house often, and her mother would cook us lavish breakfasts with sausages and eggs and toast, nothing like the dietetic fare I got at Aunt Pearl's, like cantaloupe and cottage cheese.

One day Teri came home with me to do our homework together, and Aunt Pearl's face registered horror. After Teri left, Aunt Pearl told me Teri was never allowed to sleep over at their house, simply because she was Black. I'd never known anyone like Aunt Pearl before, and it perplexed me after growing up in a home with progressive politics. My father had been a member of the Rodeo Drive Radicals and a colleague of Langston Hughes. What was I doing here? I intended to tattle on Pearl the next time I saw my father, although I knew his beliefs would not get Pearl to change her sleepover policy.

Aunt Pearl didn't forbid me from sleeping at Teri's, which I was grateful for. Teri's house was an oasis compared to the emptiness of Pearl and Alfred's. She had books and posters and records and lived like a normal fourteen-year-old. Her mother worked full time as a nurse and didn't spend her days at home wringing her hands in worry like Aunt Pearl did.

Every Wednesday was weigh-in day at my aunt and

uncle's house. If I weighed more than ninety-five pounds, I was not permitted to get my allowance or see my father. I became fixated on weigh-ins and obsessed with regaining power over my body. On Saturday mornings, when Pearl slept late, Janis and I would go up to the corner liquor store and buy candy. My favorites were Snickers bars, SweeTARTS, Good & Plenty, Red Hots, and Abba-Zabas. I'd carry my loot home and hide it from Pearl, gorging myself in secret. I'd drink diet sodas and eat less during the week, ensuring that I came in under ninety-five pounds on Wednesdays. The candy gave me my only sense of power at Pearl's, and I yearned for the private afternoons I'd spent with Michael doing whatever I wanted with my body.

In the presence of my aunt and uncle, I became more acutely aware of the absence of my maternal grandparents. My grandmother had been dead for four years, and I assumed my grandfather was living somewhere on his own. He had not communicated with me and my father since we'd left for Europe, whether because he wanted nothing to do with us or couldn't write in English, I never knew. I repeatedly asked my aunt and uncle where my grandfather was and when we would see him, and an uncomfortable pause always ensued.

"He's busy," was the usual reply.

Finally, after I'd lived with Pearl and Alfred for a few weeks, Janis told me the truth. Grandpa was in jail at Chino State Prison. Apparently this quiet, supposedly gentle man lost his shit and hauled off and knocked his second wife unconscious with a hammer. He was due back at Aunt Pearl's within the year, but I never saw him again. I attended Grandpa's funeral three years later, which is more than I got to do for my grandmother. He must have died of shame, the poor man, and yet my sympathy was tempered by the fact that he too could be abusive. No man seemed immune to it.

Riding in the back seat of Uncle Alfred's car one day, I was telling a friend that my grandfather was at Chino. "He stabbed his wife," I elaborated, "twenty-two times." I don't know where I got this information.

My Uncle Alfred hissed in his thick Viennese accent, "It vass a hammah, not a scissors! A hammah!" I stood corrected.

After a few months at Aunt Pearl's, I moved to Ojai, just south of Santa Barbara, to attend a private boarding school, Ojai Valley School. OVS was a place for Hollywood industry kids, similar to the Chadwick School and Camp Idyllwild, which I had attended five years earlier. Now I was fourteen and a cheerleader for the soccer team. One of our infamous cheers was, "Pork chops, pork chops, greasy greasy; we're gonna beat them easy easy!" Another was, "Rah rah ree, kick 'em in the knee! Rah rah rass, kick 'em in the other knee!" Soccer is not an easy game to cheer for, as there are long swaths of time with no one scoring. The cheerleading squad used to dissipate and lie in the meadow on the side of the field, some already experimenting with smoking weed. I didn't try it; I had never even gotten drunk although I was allowed to drink alcohol with my meals in Europe.

At OVS we had to wear uniforms, but we had some choices in color. We always had white shirts, but skirts and sweaters could be navy, gray, or red wool. The school was co-ed, so boys had the same choice of sweater colors, but only blue or gray pants. We slept two girls to a room in the dorms, and I still had my nighttime panic attacks, thinking about sleep and death. Now I was obsessed with my body, the pounding of my heart, what death would be like, when it would come. If I went to sleep, what if I never woke up? It is apparently a very common existential fear that millions of people experience as they fall asleep or as they try to. But I felt alone and scared. My roommate tried to console me by playing the Beach Boys *Pet Sounds* on her record player, with the volume really low after lights out. It helped, but after she fell asleep, I felt the void start to suck me down.

We took our meals in the dining hall, two rows with six long tables in each row, and it was there that I was turned against tuna salad for life. It must have been a bad batch with salmonella in the mayonnaise, and by nightfall I was in the bathroom stall puking my guts up. Fourteen times. I had nothing better to do than lie on the cool linoleum floor of the bathroom, vomit, and count. Now I can't even smell a can of tuna being opened without wanting to retch.

OVS had a small rectangular swimming pool, in ground, cement. Nothing like the lush Olympic-sized pool at Chadwick with its competitive swim team. This was more for recreation on hot days. Some of the ninth-grade boys had made it their goal to "finger" the girls while we were in the pool. The girls knew it was juvenile and intrusive, but no one knew what to do about it. It hadn't happened to me yet, but I knew if it did, the boy was going to regret it. And sure enough, one hot day I was in the pool with my new blue and yellow bathing suit when I saw a boy's form swim quickly between my legs and suddenly poke his finger up into my bathing suit bottom. He stood up sputtering and grinning in front of me, and I raised my knee as rapidly and as hard as I could between his legs. He doubled over, howling in pain.

"What did you do that for?" he whined. What did I do that for? Was he serious? Did he think I enjoyed being molested? What was wrong with him? Me, a young woman of the world? I now thought boys his age were idiots.

After half a year at OVS, my father moved up to Ojai to live and let me come stay with him and attend public high school, which I preferred. And which I am sure he preferred since it was free. I knew we did not have much money left after our three years abroad and that my father was living on his pension. I finished the tenth grade at Nordhoff Union High School.

We lived on a defunct orchid ranch called Rancho Rinconada. There was a main street like a Hollywood set, with façades of a saloon, a hotel, and general store. Each of these façades opened onto a greenhouse, once someone's dream of a huge orchid nursery covering about two acres behind the false fronts. All that was left was the white curved roofs and raised empty tables where plants had once grown.

There were three houses on the property, in addition to the fake main street, and all three were occupied. A family with two kids lived in one of the houses, and I sometimes babysat for them. A local Ojai policewoman named Lou lived in the house nearest ours, and then there was me and my father.

One morning I got up to get ready for school, which entailed walking a mile up the long driveway from the ranch to the school bus stop. I asked my father, who was still sleeping, if he wanted a cup of tea. He didn't answer. I asked again, and still no answer. I shook him, but he didn't respond. I panicked and ran next door to Lou's house, pounded on her door until she answered, and told her my father might be dead. He was unresponsive. She ran back to my house with me and into my father's bedroom.

"Charles?" Lou said loudly.

His eyes popped open.

"Yes?" he answered innocently.

"Thank God you're all right. Julietta thought there was something wrong when she couldn't wake you."

"Oh, that kid. She doesn't shut up. She yammers at me all the time and I just turn a deaf ear to her. That's all."

"Okay," Lou said as she shook her head in disbelief. I was relieved to have someone be sympathetic to me.

"Daddy, I'm going to be late for the school bus now, can you get up and drive me? I'll miss the bus."

"Not now," he said. "Maybe later, after I have my breakfast."

"I'll give you a ride," said Lou. "I'm due in for my shift soon, and the high school is on my way."

I mumbled thanks and was profoundly embarrassed to have bothered her. I was profoundly embarrassed to be dropped off at school in a police car. And I was profoundly embarrassed that my father considered me such a pest that he played dead, which was just a sick, cruel trick. I couldn't wait to live on my own and be rid of him.

Summer arrived and my father announced that he would be sending me to Queens, New York, to live with my mother's brother Dave and his wife Rose. I didn't know my aunt and uncle well but moving in with them turned out to be a gift. They were bright, fun, funny, and loved their three daughters (two of whom had married and moved out). Their youngest daughter, Vicki, was twenty-two and still lived at home, and they had room in their house (and hearts) for one more girl.

Uncle Dave was a pharmacist and went to work every day. Aunt Rose was a retired teacher who did the *New York Times* crossword puzzle in pen. She taught me to play Scrabble and the piano. Aunt Rose let me paint the radiators in my room and my cousin's room into turquoise animal shapes. My steamer trunk, which came with me from California, became my dresser, and I painted it lime green with royal blue daisies all over it. My cousin, Vicki, was in a computer programming training school, and she went off to study every day. She had a boyfriend, Robert, so she was rarely home but off driving in her white 1967 Mustang. If I was lucky, she'd take me on a "caper" with her and we'd drive off somewhere, maybe to go bowling or to White Castle for "belly burgers," or to visit Wendy, Uncle Saul's daughter, at her apartment. Wendy was married and had a two-year-old daughter, Jill, who I sometimes babysat.

Aunt Rose encouraged my independence. She arranged for a volunteer job for me at UNICEF, in New York City, stuffing holiday cards in boxes and readying them for the buying season. To get from Queens to New York City, I took the Q44A on the corner of 212th Street and Union Turnpike, then the 7 train into the city from Forest Hills. Alone! I also attended a life drawing class at the Arts Students League on 57th Street. I was trusted and valued and included and had not felt so loved since my mother had been alive.

I had never experienced such heat and humidity in my life as I did in a New York City summer. We didn't have central air conditioning, so Aunt Rose put an ancient contraption in my room that had a space for a block of ice and a fan that blew the coolness from the ice onto me. My cousin's room had an air conditioner in her window, so often I hid out in there with her, listening to records or playing my guitar. Vicki would put half-eaten sandwiches in her night table drawer, she'd pile her clothes up in her closet until the door didn't close; her room was a minefield of shoes and clothes and records and books. And I loved it. It was a place I could let go of having to control my environment—my color-coordinated underwear and socks, my shoes neatly lined up in my closet, my bed made with the sheets folded back exactly parallel to the bottom of the bed —and relax into the chaos. I believe that a certain level of security and comfort allows someone to let go like that, in a way that I could not, had not, still cannot, since I'd lost my mother. Vicki was confident in the knowledge that her parents loved her, would be there for her, and she could breathe a sigh of relief as she dropped her sweater to the floor or threw a bra to the end of her bed. I envy this ability even today, as much as I treasure the order in my own life.

I finished my last year and a half of high school living with my aunt and uncle. It was the most stability I had in seven years. I attended Martin Van Buren High School with nearly two thousand other kids, and there were so many of us that we had to attend school in three shifts. Mine was the 7:00 a.m. to 1:00 p.m. shift, which was a ridiculous and punishing time for a teenager to be awake, particularly for one who had had stayed up until 1:00 a.m. the night before watching *The Tonight Show*, which Vicki and I did every night.

I hardly got much classroom time in over that year-

and-a-half period. John Lindsay was mayor of New York City and under his watch there were three teacher strikes (one of them lasting seven months), a Broadway strike, a sanitation strike, and a blizzard that shut down the city for three days and almost ended his career. In Queens, twenty-one people died in the snowstorm, and the roads remained unplowed for a week.

The New York City teacher's strike resulted in my senior year lasting just a matter of weeks, from November 1968 until January 1969, when I graduated from high school a month before I turned seventeen.

I'd applied and was accepted to only one college, University of California Irvine, as an art major. I thought of Irvine because it was back in my home state of California, a little over an hour south of Los Angeles, near the coast, and I figured I'd live in the dorms and stay with my father during holidays. I still had the fantasy of being a family with my father, but in December 1968, I got a Christmas card from him telling me that he'd married Margaret Breil, the woman he had been dating for a year. They would be moving to a retirement community where the minimum age for residence was fifty-seven.

My father informed me that he would not be supporting me at college. He said that the only reason to go was to find a husband, and maybe get a degree as a nurse or teacher to have "something to fall back on" if marriage didn't work out. When I wrote my father back to ask him for some financial assistance to get started at university, he sent me a note that said, simply, "*King Lear*, Act I, Scene IV."

I went to the library, found a copy of the play, and looked it up.

"Ingratitude, thou marble-hearted fiend,
More hideous, when thou show'st thee in a child
Than the sea-monster!"

And there it was. He was done with me being his charge. My freedom was about to begin, and it terrified and thrilled me all at once.

13

SEX, DRUGS, AND ROCK 'N' ROLL

I got to Irvine in April of 1969. I had just turned seventeen. Within weeks, I'd met James, a man whom I adored. He wasn't the man I lost my virginity to though; that was either a few weeks before I started school, with the father of a kid I babysat for (but I was wearing a tampon, so I am not sure if that really counted). Or it was with my friend's cousin, also a few weeks before school started. My friend's cousin told me, "Just one thrust and it won't hurt anymore." I think it was probably him, because I bled after, and it was not much fun at all. I believe that no woman really enjoys the loss of her virginity or tries to think much about it afterward, except to note the benchmark in her life and tell her friends, "I lost my virginity." It's pretty much always disappointing. And in my case, it was dubious. Yes, I had the first penis I ever had inside me, so doesn't that count? Or does tearing a hymen count more? Which is it, and does it matter?

But sex with James was heavenly. James was darkskinned, tall, with a beard, and wore a Mao cap. He had a copy of Mao's *Little Red Book* in his back pocket and often just stood in the UCI Commons playing his saxophone. We were intensely attracted to each other.

My relationship with my father had become that of two adults, sort of—he was sixty-nine and I was seventeen —and I visited him on occasion in Leisure World, the retirement community where he and Margaret lived in Laguna Hills not far from UC Irvine. I really liked my stepmother, so I kept in touch with them. I was desperate to craft family from something that didn't really exist between us.

I wanted to see my dad, to tell him about school and all about James. I thought my father was going to be so happy for me. I was enjoying college, and I had met a sweet young man. And not only had I met a good man, he was curious about Communism. Like so many young Black men of his era, James believed that Communism was a vehicle to grant "power to the people." I thought he and my dad would have so much to talk about.

"That's YOUR misfortune!" my father shouted at me before he slammed his bedroom door. He didn't come out the rest of my visit, so my stepmother and I sat together, with her trying to console me.

I was shocked and disappointed by my father's reaction. My dad was so hip, so open-minded, so progressive. He was liberal, I thought. What exactly was this misfortune he was talking about? That James was Black? A Communist? It would be many years before I could see that he was so bitter about his life he could not let me enjoy my own happiness. The impact of McCarthyism on my father was huge, but that was not where his unhappiness began. He carried that weight from boyhood, through two pogroms and untold trauma, which may have explained his bitterness but certainly did not excuse it.

After that, he never met any of my boyfriends, not even my husband until after I'd been married for almost a year. I wouldn't let him. And I never discussed James with him again.

James and I lasted a long time by Irvine standards. He used to come to my dorm room at night, and when I moved to nearby Balboa Island in the fall of 1969, he'd drive out there in his orange VW Bus to be with me. My roommate used to laugh that she could never hear us, really, only his very deep voice making the walls rumble. He said things to me no man had ever said before, held me so tenderly, and smelled so good. I really thought this was love, but I was just seventeen.

I became aware of the racism and intense prejudice in Orange County one night when James came to visit me. He was in a horrible mood, furious, because a cop had stopped him after he crossed the bridge over to Balboa Island. And, I found out, it was not the first night a cop stopped him. Seems every time he drove over to this community of roach-infested little rental houses, he got stopped and interrogated. Driving while Black. But we didn't call it that then.

Saying that he was going to visit his girlfriend did not help his case much. The cops were white, nearly everyone on the island was white, and he was not. And he got harassed for it.

That night I truly lost my innocence. I cried in his arms, and he must have thought I was an idiot. He'd grown up with this shit his whole life. I had grown up not only in Los Angeles and New York, but also in Austria,

Italy, and Spain. And living abroad in a community of expatriates was very liberating. Since everyone was from someplace else, it was our otherness that made us feel like we belonged with each other. Consequently, religion, skin color, nationality, sexual preference even, didn't matter. Our bond was that we were all outsiders.

Not long after that night, James and I just drifted apart.

Almost everyone at Irvine was taking drugs of some kind or another, whether for fun or thrills or to relax or to expand consciousness. Although I looked like a hippie, my experience with drugs was vicarious except for the maybe five times I smoked weed or hash. If people smoked in my house, I left the house.

One time, on a rare occasion when I apparently wanted to get stoned and was not afraid to, I went to this guy Jasper's house in Verano Place. Jasper was a surfer dude. Skinny guy, buck teeth, always little bits of sand clinging to his big Afro. Goofy grin. He had copped a lid to share. An ounce then cost only five dollars. Anyway, there were too many of us to roll joints for. We were just hanging out and listening to the music he liked, bands like The Moody Blues and Blood, Sweat & Tears. Jasper put the pot on a saucer and lit it, and when it was good and smoking, he put an Indian bedspread over us all as we sat on the floor and leaned in over the saucer and inhaled. I observed my two-hit rule, and after a couple of breaths, came out from underneath and ran home to my apartment.

Unlike me, my first roommate, Lynn, loved drugs. Lynn got her hands on everything while we lived in Balboa Island. We smoked hash together using a toilet paper tube pipe and an aluminum foil bowl with holes punched in it. Lynn loved it, but I thought I was going to die and that the John Coltrane album I was listening to controlled my body, the drums my heart, and when the music stopped, I'd be done for.

Lynn snorted cocaine and told me I had to try it, that I'd love it. "It's like a cool rainforest at the back of your head," she said. But I couldn't do it.

Pretty much everyone I knew was into drugs. I did not want to acquire a reputation as a druggie, even though the assumption that I must be one was made based on how I dressed. In fact, there was an article in the *Santa Ana Register* about me, which, if I could go back and sue those bastards for libel, I would, except they didn't use my name. Just the headline "Counselor Gets Sent Home for Drug Use." I was enraged.

This is what happened. I worked as a volunteer with some junior high kids in a project meant to get the kids excited about school and learning. We went away for a weekend to a camp and had all these activities planned. But I was sick with strep, had a 103-degree fever, and I was on antibiotics. I was hoping to get better, but I reacted badly to the erythromycin, and by the end of the first day I still did not feel well. I asked the project director to find someone to replace me or to manage somehow without me. He begged me to stay, but I knew I couldn't. I was hot and dizzy. As I walked to my cabin to lie down, some women were wandering around asking questions (I had no idea they were reporters), and they stopped to talk. I told them I really couldn't, that I was sick and the drugs I was on were making me sicker, and I was hoping to get a ride back to Irvine. Maybe I even asked them if they could give me a ride.

On the following Monday, I saw the headline, and I was livid. But there was nothing I could do. It wasn't true —I was not sent home, and it wasn't the illegal drugs that they were implying—but my name was not used, just every other detail of the weekend.

My friend John thought I was a drag because of my fear of drugs. Maybe I do overreact when drugs are involved. Maybe it's my own terror of getting high that causes me to be judgmental. Maybe it's my fear of arrest, of losing people I care about. Or maybe it's jealousy that I can't get high and enjoy it. I thought that psychedelics made you have personal, impressionist paintings in your brain, and I admit I was angry with myself that I was missing out on something. I used to think if only I weren't such a chicken, I too could have kaleidoscopic, mind-expanding trips.

Anyway, my experience with drugs as a hippie did not change my life, open my heart, expand my consciousness, and remove my inhibitions. I was afraid of recreational drugs, and I still am. But for John, psychedelics were having the effect of softening him and opening him and healing him from the trauma of being in Vietnam. And he became one of my best friends at Irvine, the man to whose apartment I would hitchhike on many occasions, knock on his door, and climb into his bed and spoon with him to cry when I had been flayed emotionally by a breakup or a cheating boyfriend. John was tall, thin, and freckled, with long red hair and round John Lennon glasses. He would hold me all night and never put the moves on me, for which I was grateful. Although many years later he sent me a note saying "All those sleepovers and no loving. I wish I'd turned you around and checked out the other side."

Once John and I went over to our friend Rick's house, where Rick's Afghan hound had given birth to eight puppies. Rick's girlfriend, Miranda, was there, and John got high with them. Then we all went skinny dipping in the pool, and afterward lay naked on Rick's queen size bed with puppies crawling all over us for an hour. That's the kind of stuff that hippies did for fun. That and listen to music.

I became a true lover of jazz during my Irvine years. I had a lot to learn, but that was okay because there was a pretty big group of us who went to the jazz clubs together. There was The Lighthouse Café in Hermosa Beach, Shelly's Manne-Hole in Los Angeles, and Funky Quarters in San Diego. We went to all of them. Our group was a multi-ethnic mix of Chicanos, Italians, Puerto Ricans, Blacks, and whites united by our affinity for jazz. Some people knew more than others and turned the less knowledgeable ones of us onto new stuff. I heard Gábor Szabó, Miles Davis, Milt Jackson, and Les McCann live. I even had a little "thang" going on with Les.

It started when I saw Les and his group play at Shelly's Manne-Hole. I was wearing a black velvet, low-cut mini dress with a white lace collar. My hair was forked out about four inches all around my head in a globe of curls. I got up to go to the ladies' room, and Les altered the lyrics to one of his songs, something about it being nice to be in the "big titty, I mean big city." It got a laugh. Oh, how sexist and inappropriate it was. I was just becoming aware of feminism. When I returned to my table, my cousin, Robbie, who was with me said, "He was talking about you."

"Huh?" I asked dumbly.

"That drink," he pointed to a glass on our table that had not been there before, "is for you, from Les." He pointed to the stage. I was stunned. I'd never been flirted with so publicly before, and of course I liked it.

I went backstage with him after the show and found myself being kissed. I wasn't sure how I felt about it; I didn't know then that a girl my age, eighteen at the time, could have such a strong influence over a grown man. But I learned to appreciate it, relish it in the bigger picture of my life. I had power! Les would write to me, comp me to his shows, buy me drinks, and after all the sets, in the wee hours, I'd go back to his dressing room, and we'd fool around. I felt so privileged that he always singled me out when he played and sang to me and talked to me from the stage. Of course, I knew he probably did it to young women in every town and every club that he played at, had his whole collection of groupies, but I dug it anyway, and it lasted pretty much through my three Irvine years.

Today, I'll hear Janis Joplin's "Piece of My Heart" or "Glad" by Traffic, and it's just a historical marker, a great song but something I don't have a personal memory connected to. But to play Les's music now, from one of the albums he autographed to me, or to hear any of his music I loved then and still do, transports me back to that time, to happy memories of when I enjoyed myself, enjoyed my newfound sense of agency and power and was not fearful.

In December 1971, I found myself in the university infirmary. For days I had tried dragging myself to class, staying awake through lectures, and dragging myself back home again, but to no avail. I couldn't keep myself awake. I was hospitalized with mononucleosis and spent four days in the infirmary, mostly sleeping.

One evening my Nigerian roommate, Funmilayo, came whooshing into my hospital room in her gorgeous dress and headwrap, layers of blues and greens and yellows, carrying the Mexican candelabra I had purchased on one of my trips to Tijuana. It was blue with flowers and vines and dots and lines and had holders for eight candles. She also brought a box of little colored candles and a box of matches.

"It's the first night of Hanukkah!" Funmilayo exclaimed. "It's your holiday! You have to light the candles." I was touched by her consideration, even though I had never celebrated Hanukkah in my life, much less knew how to light Hanukkah candles or say any blessings. I thanked Funmilayo, who stayed with me for a bit until my eyes began to close again. She sat in the corner, just like my mother had when I woke up from my adenoid surgery. Only this time there was no Chinese food.

When I awoke, I was alone in my dark infirmary room, with only the light of a streetlamp coming through the window. I thought about when I was little, how I was terrified of the dark, but my mother refused to buy me a night-light. Instead, she put a candle on my antique nightstand. But to emphasize the dangers of fire, she took my index finger and passed it through the flame, so I would know how it felt to get burned.

"You see, Julietta? That's why you have to be very careful of fire. It can really hurt you," she said as the blister was forming. Then she kissed me goodnight and left the room.

I placed the makeshift menorah on the hospital table next to my bed, inserted eight colored candles, and lit them. My first Hanukkah.

I had always had what I thought was a healthy fear of fire, including of the pilot flame on the gas water heater at the countess's house in Treviso, but these little candles were comforting and made me feel less alone.

I promised myself that I would call the synagogue in Newport Beach when I was discharged and ask them to tell me about the prayers for candle lighting. Back in my apartment with Funmilayo and our other two roommates, for the remaining Hanukkah nights I read the prayers from a little scrap of paper as I lit each candle. I learned that to do it properly you needed to place each candle in the menorah from right to left and then light them left to right using a ninth candle, the *shamash*. For now, a match would have to do.

Baruch atah Adonai, Eloheinu Melech ha'olam, asher kid'shanu b'mitzvotav, v'tzivanu, l'hadlik ner, shel Hanukkah.

A commandment to light the lights. Look but not touch. Let there be light.

"*Ah Freilichin Hanukkah, klayneleh,*" I imagined Grandpa Joseph saying.

14

OUR BODIES, OURSELVES

I graduated from UC Irvine in three years, in a big hurry to get out and live on my own as an adult. My third and final year at Irvine, 1972, I had a part-time job working for an abortion clinic. I drove a van that had "Pregnant?" and a phone number written on both sides of it, and I would park it at the beach and walk up and down the sand handing out condoms and answering questions about birth control and abortion, which was legal in California. I also translated a lot of the clinic's brochures into Spanish. My facility with languages may be a gift or may have to do with the fact that I learned those five languages when I was a child. I don't know. But whatever language I speak, I seem to have mastered the native pronunciation and can do a more than passable job at translation.

During my college years, my consciousness was being raised in terms of who made decisions about our bodies when we became pregnant. But it wasn't only the decision to be pregnant or not. We were getting more militant about whether to have sex or not, and with whom. Which is why when I was bamboozled and raped by a boyfriend's roommate I was infuriated.

I remember my rape vividly. It was around ten o'clock at night. I went to my boyfriend's apartment to meet him after his long drive home from Oakland to Irvine. His roommate told me he was napping in the next room and would be awake shortly, to have a seat on the couch and wait. Naively, I did. A part of me felt I shouldn't be in this guy's apartment possibly alone with him at this hour, but I stayed. I remember that Roberta Flack's "The First Time Ever I Saw Your Face" was playing when this tall, handsome man grabbed me and began kissing me. (It's hard to believe, but I can't remember the name of my then-boyfriend or the name of the man who raped me. Does that mean I was more traumatized than I think? Or less so because it is fading into the gossamer of memory?) I pushed him away, and he thrust my head against the wooden back of the couch. I began to punch him, I slammed my fist upwards into his balls, I bit his hand, and he yelped and reacted with force. He ripped my pants down, tearing one of my leather sandal straps in the process, and pulled my shirt so hard the buttons popped off, exposing my bare breasts. As he shoved me back onto the couch, I gave up and went into freeze mode. As he shoved his hard penis into me, my mind left my body and I hummed inside my head to Roberta Flack still playing on the stereo. Within minutes, he had come, and to my surprise I felt him sobbing an apology into my neck, "I'm so sorry. So sorry. I'm high on angel dust. Please, please forgive me."

I didn't reply. I clutched my shirt closed over my breasts with one hand, held onto my broken sandals with the other, and raced out of the apartment barefoot, leaving him sitting on the couch, embarrassed. I was blind with anger and shame. I limped back to my third-floor apartment across the landscaped paths through Verano Place. None of my roommates were home, and I showered and went to bed, falling into a deep sleep.

The next day I saw my friend Chrissie and I told her that I had been raped. To my surprise, Chrissie said, "He raped me, too." We both felt that there was no point in trying to prosecute him. We worried that because neither of us were virgins and we had undoubtedly worn provocative clothing (which is to say either pants or a dress, as both were considered provocative), we would be told we had "asked for it" by being in a man's apartment at night or had unintentionally invited sexual advances by just being female. As far as we were concerned, men always got away with it.

This is not to say we weren't devastated by it. Chrissie never shared all the details of her violation with me. But she didn't have to. We commiserated with each other and mended ourselves. We were resilient and strong, or as strong as we could be for two twenty-year-olds.

We weren't so much angry that this creep had fucked us as we were furious that we didn't say he could. After the shock of having the clothes ripped off our bodies and of our powerlessness against a six-foot-three man had worn off, we were able to console ourselves and each other. The rape did not affect my ability to trust men, basically because I don't really and never did, thanks to my father's admonitions that men only wanted one thing. So be it, I thought, and here that thing is, have at it. But rape was violence, an assault. It was not sex, even though there was a penis inside my vagina. What I got out of consensual sex was a feeling of closeness, of safety, of being embraced and desired for as long as the naked lasted, and it felt good. Rape was not that.

As I learned more about sex and power and my body from real life, I took courses in human sexuality and learned at the clinic where I worked about all the different types of birth control available. I watched videos of vasectomies. I held women's hands as they had abortions. I learned how to put a speculum inside me and look at my cervix in a mirror. I was owning my parts, and I was teaching other women how to own theirs.

After I graduated, I had the opportunity to move to Montreal, where I worked in a women's center, taught courses in human sexuality, ran consciousness-raising groups, and began to live my life as an independent young adult. I was involved in starting a rape crisis center (or centre, as it was spelled there) in Montreal, with a badass group of feminists. As it was getting off the ground, in the dead of a mortifyingly cold winter where your nose hairs freeze as you inhale, I took a vacation to warm Guadalajara, Mexico, and there my history changed.

I befriended some white, blond college kids from Washington state who invited me to share their apartment with them in a lovely, verdant, whitewashed neighborhood in Guadalajara in exchange for my translation services. I was sunbathing topless when a handsome, tall, tanned, and bearded young man came into the courtyard. I looked up and noted he was wearing a straw hat against the potent sun, and I also noted that he was not wearing underwear beneath his ragged-edged cutoff shorts. We fell in lust with each other. His name was Bill, and he was from White

Plains, New York. He was driving around Mexico with his two friends, one of whom was in medical school in Guadalajara.

Bill and I ate dinner at Carlos O'Willys, and he paid. He was the first man who'd ever bought me dinner, and I was impressed with his generosity. Then we went to see the movie *Shaft*, dubbed in Spanish. Rats nibbled popcorn on the floor around the movie theater's seats, and I kept my legs folded in my lap through the entire show. We went back to the apartment where I was staying, and we slept together. He was the first man I had an orgasm with. I took it as a sign. God, I was naïve.

Bill and I moved in with each other a year later, into a 140-year-old farmhouse in Silver Lake, New York, just north of White Plains. A few months after we started living together, we were married at the town hall in Harrison, New York, by a justice of the peace. Then we went out for Szechuan food to celebrate.

I married to become part of a family, to realize all my dreams of belonging. But Bill's upbringing was nothing like mine. He was raised in the suburbs and went to elementary, middle, high school, and Hebrew school all in White Plains. Even though there was rage and dysfunction in his family, they still were much like a traditional nuclear family. Maybe even with the rage and dysfunction?

I never did belong in his family; I was just too odd for them. Our value systems clashed, and I know it was a source of discomfort for Bill to be an intermediary between his wife and his family of birth. Yes, there were family gatherings, but I constantly felt left out even in a crowd of his people, where there was always a slight haze of dislike for me hanging over everything. Once again, I was an "other," never fully accepted.

Bill attended SUNY Purchase while I worked for the Westchester Department of Mental Health, driving to Peekskill every day. I had my own caseload of Spanish-speaking teenage clients, whom I counseled as best I could and provided with information on human sexuality. Bill and I were great as roommates, almost like siblings, but there was never wild passion in our relationship, at least not in our lovemaking. The only time Bill was passionate was when he was angry, and it terrified me. I learned to soothe his anger, or anticipate it so that he would not explode, and we learned to live with each other.

Two years after we were married, I discovered I was pregnant. My diaphragm had failed as a contraceptive, but I was happy about the surprise. However, Bill's reaction to my news was simply, "Oh." He wanted me to have an abortion, but I knew I couldn't do that, even if it was legal to do so. This was a baby that I created with a man I loved, and although I was frightened because we weren't sure how we would manage financially, I was excited beyond imagination to become a mother, to rectify all the things that had been mishandled in my childhood. When an elderly woman in her eighties, a cousin of my husband's named Regina, told me not to be fearful, that "babies bring their own luck," I relaxed into my pregnancy and so did Bill.

I became adamant that reproductive freedom did not just mean the right to terminate a pregnancy. It also meant the right to give birth the way I wanted, and where I wanted, and with whom. And my only option in Westchester County, New York, was in a hospital with a doctor and drugs.

I think the idea of being drugged scared me more than the idea of being in a hospital, though that fear was close behind. Women were making a lot of noise about natural childbirth, but I couldn't find anywhere that would allow me to have an unmedicated birth. And the idea of being "allowed" to do something with my own body enraged me. It was my body and my choice, and now I was on the other end of the spectrum of reproductive freedom.

We found out that there was a doctor in Los Angeles who had a staff of midwives who caught babies (not "delivered" them) in his office, in rooms with double beds. Partners could be present, so could friends and other family members. We had never heard of this before, but it sounded wonderful and exactly like what we wanted. We packed up and drove to Los Angeles to give birth at the Natural Childbirth Institute.

Our white German shepherd, Kif, accompanied us, as did our two cats, Lizzie and Willis. The car reeked of litter box, and Bill had to pull over often for me to puke out the car door. I was nauseated all nine months of that pregnancy. It was awful. I drank raspberry leaf tea and ginger tea but just about everything came back up.

In LA, we moved into an apartment on Mayfield Avenue, where our rude landlady called me "Fatty" until I gave birth. I don't think she ever knew my real name even though it was on the check we gave her every month. Bill, who had dropped out of school to support us, got a job in the lighting department at Bullock's department store.

We began attending weekly natural childbirth classes, and what I learned was how little, up to that point, I really knew about pregnancy and birth. I studied how babies developed in utero, when the gender was determined, when first kicks could be felt, and what was happening to my body as my uterus grew. Dizziness, fatigue, heartburn, constipation, and swollen ankles—all normal, thank you very much.

My pregnancy was completely low risk, and I was able to give birth in the birth center, with Bill there, the midwife, our childbirth educator (as what we would now call a doula), and two friends, one of whom brought her three week old who'd also been born there. It was an intense, openhearted experience and I never once felt out of control. This was my body doing magic. Our son, Noah, was healthy, and we were overjoyed to be parents.

Noah's birth empowered me so much that I wanted to spread the word that births like this were not only possible but desirable. All the medical bells and whistles were available in case of emergency, and the hospital was just a few blocks away. I felt safe and strong. As far as I was concerned, birth centers or homes were the only places to have babies. Hospitals should be a last resort for women who needed surgical births or had other complications requiring medical intervention.

And, oh, how I loved this baby. I loved that he took his nourishment from my body. Now I understood why my mother had breastfed me even though it was uncommon in the 1950s. It was joy to have that closeness, to be so connected, and to be keeping another human alive. It was a joy to touch his soft skin, to wonder at his fingers and toes, and become the smitten-with-love cliché you read about and think, naively, "Nah, I'm not going to be like that." Yet there we were, marveling at the tiny crescents of

Noah's fingernails and rejoicing at the number of soiled diapers he produced. Of course, there were many days I was bleary from little sleep and wished only to be able to stay late in bed, eat when I wanted to, and have a cup of tea that was still hot when I drank it. But Bill was there to help me most of the time, and he was a caring and involved father.

My career path became clear to me: I knew that I wanted to inspire pregnant women to have the kinds of births they wanted, to feel the power that I had, to become mothers in the same tender and loving way. Motherhood changed me, unlocked me, allowed me to become nurturing and wholeheartedly caring even though I had not experienced it myself. I wondered how it was possible to overcome the multiple little and big abandonments I had experienced to live in the wet bliss of motherhood, but I had. Where I had been wildly unmothered, I wanted to give mothers and babies the best, most loving starts to their lives, to create bonds that would help mitigate any future losses like divorce or death of a parent. I knew my idea wasn't a panacea that would ensure good attachment, but it was a bold start to women's journeys as mothers.

Not only did I enjoy this part of my life, I wanted to shout about it. I wanted to enable other women to have the agency to fulfill their own choices regarding birth. I was going to become a childbirth educator, attend births, maybe even become a midwife. When Bill and I drove back to New York from Los Angeles in 1978, I knew that I'd have to start a birth center myself if I wanted to give birth in one in Westchester County, New York.

In addition to being certain about my career path, I was also certain that I wanted to give whatever children I birthed the kind of stability that I never had, so I chose to work only part-time to be able to be at home and raise my kids. Three years after my son was born, I gave birth to a strong baby girl, Miriam, in a birth center in New York City, assisted by a midwife and caught by her father, with two of my dearest friends in attendance. I knew I wanted to dedicate my life to being the best mother I could.

I was born in an in-between generation—where women of my mother's generation had pretty much all gotten married and stayed home (my mother gave up her job as a theatrical agent when she married my father), the women of my daughter's generation pretty much all work, whether or not they are raising families. My father urged me to forego college and find a husband, but I wanted to do both, be married and work. And I wanted to work, but on my terms, so I could also be present with my children. I was not going to choose between them and my career, nor was I going to give up my dream of starting a birth center or of staying connected to pregnancy and birth the rest of my life. And so, my life's work began.

When I was twenty-six, my dad came to New York to visit me, Bill, and baby Noah. When I prepared to go out one evening to see my therapist, my father snapped, "What do you need a therapist for?!"

"Daddy, I did not have the easiest childhood," I said, as diplomatically as I could.

"You have these fantasies growing in your head like a cancer! You should get them excised."

I had been on my own almost a decade at that point and with it came much-needed perspective. Pretending that loss did not exist was not a coping mechanism I was interested in. I walked out the door without a word.

In 1979, I sat at my kitchen table in New York having coffee with my friend Dena. I had received my certification and was teaching childbirth education classes as well as attending the births of some of my clients as a doula. Working as a doula, I was able to provide support through delivery and the fourth trimester, the early weeks of parenthood. I was empowering parents and supporting them while they gave birth. It was fulfilling but it wasn't enough for me.

I wanted people to have the birth experience that I had in LA. Many people were still arguing with their physicians for the right to have a natural birth. Everything was a battle, but it didn't need to be. Birth should be a happy, welcoming event instead of a struggle for permission to make choices about one's own body. Historically, women's concerns are not heard in healthcare settings, and I wanted them to know I heard their concerns, and a good birth was possible.

With Noah toddling at my feet, I said to Dena, "I want there to be a birth center here. I want to have my next baby at a birth center." Shifting the baby on her lap, Dena looked at me and replied, "Let's figure out how to make that happen." And we did. We made a business plan on the kitchen table, mapping out my ideas and crunching numbers. Soon I had the blueprint for what I wanted to do next.

I had the great good fortune of having an active partner to help parent our kids. Bill was in school to get a teaching degree, and I attended graduate school at night for my master's degree in health administration. We took turns shopping and cooking, taking the kids to the pediatrician, and until he began to work full-time, it was an equitable arrangement. By then our kids were in school and I was freer to pursue the founding of the birth center.

With a group of fellow professionals, I formed a not-for-profit board of talented volunteers from various disciplines (midwifery, law, marketing, fundraising, education, politics, and medicine), which lobbied the pertinent people and agencies, including the New York State Department of Health (DOH). I was its director, and we were supported by community members, Maternity Center Association in New York City (where my daughter was born), the National Association of Childbearing Centers, the Jacob Burns Foundation, and several individuals and non-profit organizations.

But we were also ridiculed. A doctor at a hearing for the DOH, upon learning of our fundraising attempts, wagged a dollar bill in our faces. Midwives did not even have hospital privileges yet in Westchester County. Hospitals refused to back us and accept our transfers, with one doctor saying, "We are not taking over when you send us women bleeding to death," despite the excellent statistics on midwifery care. Finding a location seemed futile, since we needed money to afford a home where births could happen, but donors were reluctant to give us money if we didn't have the location. My associate director, Ellen Rubin, and I were even mocked by our own husbands, who called us Lucy and Ethel and said the birth center was nothing but a pipedream.

From 1979 to 1993 we struggled, pushed, gave up our dream, returned to it, disbanded the board, and brought it back for one final gasp. In 1991, we decided to partner with a hospital or health center and transfer our Certificate of Need (CON) to an agency that already had DOH approval and collaborate. We settled on Hudson Valley Hospital in Peekskill, and the birth center, the Birth Cottage, was finally opened in January of 1994. I would be its executive director, but instead of my having the autonomy I had dreamed of, there was a director of nursing and a hospital administrator above me. It was the only way we could see to open and give women in Westchester an alternative to hospital birth.

Once the birth center was successful, I felt bored and hated to be working for the straight, radically conservative administration at Hudson Valley Hospital. On one occasion, in a closed staff meeting, the hospital administrator told the secretary to stop recording the meeting. Then he warned us to tell all our hospital suppliers that unless they voted for the Republican candidate for New York governor, we would no longer order from them. I was disgusted. Add to that the fact that I had insomnia, eczema, and had lost fifteen pounds, and I decided I needed to look for work somewhere else. I was pretty sure the birth center could run without me, and I knew that Ellen would stay there looking out for the birth center's best interests.

When I received a call from the national headquarters of March of Dimes asking if I wanted to start their resource center, I jumped at the opportunity. I love creating things, but I get antsy sticking with them once they are running smoothly. A new project was just the excitement I needed.

I remained in that role for over a year, getting the resource center launched and then renowned, when Maternity Center Association (the first birth center in the United States and where I had given birth to my daughter years earlier) recruited me to oversee the Early Discharge

Program that New York's DOH had asked them to spearhead.

In the mid-1990s, insurance companies stopped reimbursing for days-long maternity stays and capped their payments at forty-eight hours following birth. This mandate caused quite a scandal at the time, and many people saw early discharge as "drive-by deliveries." But those of us in the birth center world felt that returning home as soon as possible after a birth made the most sense, as parents could begin their journeys as new families without the medicalized intrusion of hospital staff and procedures. We knew that with proper discharge procedures and clinical benchmarks, moms and babies could safely return home within hours of birth without any detriment.

New York State's DOH knew that the premier birth center in the country, Maternity Center Association, had written the book on early discharge protocols and asked us to bring hospitals into alignment with those practices. As director of early discharge programming, I began to meet with hospital labor and delivery units and to lecture around the tri-state area.

I was driving down the Garden State Parkway on a beautiful October day to present MCA's guidelines at a maternal infant health conference in Atlantic City, New Jersey. As I exited a toll plaza and was just beginning to gather speed, I was rear-ended by a car going almost sixty miles an hour. My car's wheels left the road, and my car spun a 180-degree turn in the air, finally landing to the side of the center guardrail. I was in shock when the police showed up, in shock in the ambulance, and numbed into silence in the ER waiting for Bill to come and get me. I was so scrambled that when the cop showed up with the purse I had left in my car, I thought he owned a purse just like mine. When Bill arrived, I apologized to him for the car accident, even though it was not my fault. I feared what the repairs would cost us, although I should not have worried. The car was totaled, and I would win the lawsuit against the woman who had hit me. (She was arrested trying to leave the scene of the accident.)

But that was not the end of it. I kept mixing up words or forgetting them. I suddenly had a hair-trigger temper and had no issue cursing out store managers and bank tellers and anyone who pissed me off. I lost my short-term memory. I couldn't add numbers. At night, in my sleep, I sometimes tried to crawl out our bedroom window to safety. I was clearly emotionally traumatized, in addition to the constant neck and back pain I suffered.

I returned to work. But I would just stare at my computer and not know what to do, how to sequence my tasks, or make sense of the million-dollar budget I oversaw. I was struggling and I was ashamed of it. After extensive neurological and psychological testing, I was told that I had suffered a mild but permanent brain injury. I had problems with executive functions (ergo my impulsivity and short temper), information processing and sequencing, dyscalculia or trouble doing arithmetic calculations, auditory processing and word-finding problems, and issues with short-term memory. I would be a slower, more tentative version of myself for the rest of my life.

Two years of twice-weekly neuropsychological rehabilitation ensued, and although I learned techniques for compensating or coping with my brain injury, my life further unraveled. Bill apparently could not handle having a wife with a brain injury and began sleeping with a close family friend. I knew the affair was going on, I just *sensed* it, but each time I confronted him, he told me I was crazy and overly jealous with a fantastical imagination. I had begun to doubt everything else in my life, so I convinced myself to believe my husband when I shouldn't have.

Eventually, with the help of friends who worked at Bill's school, we tracked down the apartment that he and our family friend used to conduct their affair. I told a teacher friend to meet Bill in the morning when he arrived at school and tell him his affair had been uncovered. It was at that point that he finally admitted that he had been cheating on me, for a year and a half. I changed the locks and put his belongings in the driveway.

We sold our house and got divorced. I moved into my own little cottage in nearby Mount Kisco, New York, and began a life as a single empty nester. I was incredibly lonely and not sure what to do with myself. Although I dated several lovers whom I met through online services, relationships felt hollow, and I decided to press pause on dating for a while. I spent a few years enriching my friendships with the women in my life, gardening, singing in a choir, and staying in contact with my college-aged children. It pained me that my marriage had failed, that our children did not have a family home to return to, that my ex had a partner, and that I was alone when I felt I most needed a shoulder to lean on. I felt abandoned, again, even though I had just turned fifty.

15

LAND OF MY FATHERS

Turning fifty was unnerving. I was terrified that I would die at that age, as my mother had. It was not a rational fear, but I was worried that my genes were poisoned, or they had some kind of use-by date that would sneak up on me and kill me. My therapist was constantly reassuring me that I was not my mother, that I didn't smoke cigarettes as she had (let alone two packs a day), and that I was not a candidate for a heart attack. I had started medication for depression and panic disorder after my brain injury was diagnosed, and it helped a lot. But the fear was still there, a constant passenger in my subconscious, like an unwelcome hitchhiker. A hitchhiker who smoked with the windows rolled up.

Was I like my mother at all? Yes, I believed in organic food, and I believed in breastfeeding. But I sure as hell did not believe in Waldorf education or wrapping raw onions around my child's neck to treat an illness. I did not have a big, loud family around me like my mother did, my children did not have involved grandparents like I had with my mother's parents, and there were no Passover seders.

When I was first married, I had tried to serve a Passover meal to my husband. I made a brisket and *charoset* (an apple-walnut mixture that is supposed to resemble the mortar the Israelites used to construct buildings in Egypt), and bought matzos, and created a small seder plate with all the ritual foods on it. I set a festive table with spring flowers and colorful napkins. My husband walked over to our table and said, "What is this shit?!" and I told him it was a Passover meal. He tolerated it, but I did not do anything like that again until our kids were born, and we agreed that they needed some kind of religious education.

Growing up, Bill had been tortured with Hebrew school four days a week, and his parents attended an Orthodox synagogue with his paternal grandparents. Bill eschewed all that as soon as he had his bar mitzvah. I had no real Jewish upbringing, and though I went to church throughout my early childhood I didn't feel Christian either. We decided to join a Reform synagogue when Noah was five and Miriam was two to create some traditions for our children. What we loved about the synagogue was that the rabbi would tell stories, and the kids would sit in the carpeted aisles playing with toys and feeling welcomed by the congregation. It was a far cry from Bill's strict, Orthodox upbringing and my eclectic Judeo-Christian one. It suited us, and it was there that I learned to chant the prayers and sing the songs, and I learned their meanings as opposed to just repeating transliterated words as I had with my first Hanukkah in Irvine all those years before.

My interest in Judaism also led to my being a part of a Jewish community as my children went to Hebrew school and studied for their bar and bat mitzvahs. Bill and I attended social and educational events at our synagogue. In 1993, we met a Torah scribe who had come to repair the synagogue's Torah. It had been recovered from Nazi pillaging in a town called Brno in the former Czechoslovakia. The Torah dated back to 1838 and had been cleaned and repaired before, at least once. Now the black Hebrew letters were beginning to chip off again. The congregants were invited to place a hand over the scribe's as he inked in a letter that corresponded to the congregant's name. I placed my hand over his as he wrote an aleph (the letter a in Hebrew), and I was incredibly moved to be part of my culture's history.

The scribe had lived the hippie lifestyle in San Francisco and caught the religion bug when his wife came home one day and announced that she was embracing her Jewish roots. He was surprised but gradually became more and more religious as her newfound interests appealed more and more to him. He had studied art in college and applied his art background to learning how a Torah was written. He learned Hebrew, and by the time I met him he could read from and identify any part of the five books of the Torah (Genesis, Exodus, Leviticus, Numbers, and Deuteronomy).

I asked the scribe if he needed an apprentice, told him that I had studied art in college, and to my surprise he said yes.

I took the train to his Manhattan studio in June 1993, on a hot sticky day. First, the scribe taught me how to clean the Torah using a drafting dry-cleaning bag, a bag filled with pulverized gum eraser granules. By gently rubbing the Torah with it, one can remove smudges and smears and some stains. For the more difficult stains I was shown how to carefully use denatured alcohol. After two days of using the dry-cleaning pad, he asked me if I was ready to fill in some chipped letters. As nervous as I was, I still said yes. The outlines of all the chipped and faded letters were still there, so I traced over them using the traditional quill and gall wasp ink. The resulting color dried to a thick, shiny black. I was complimented on the precision of my work and urged to continue on my own, rolling and unrolling the Torah as I progressed.

On the third day of my apprenticeship, the scribe came in with our lunches and sat down.

"I have something to tell you," he said. "I waited until now because I didn't want to make you nervous."

"What?" I asked, taking a bite of my fruit salad. "You're making me nervous now."

"You are the first woman in history to repair a Torah."

I swallowed my cantaloupe cube and stared at him.

"Are you serious? I'm glad you didn't tell me before. My hand would have been shaking!"

"I know. There were probably daughters of scribes in the olden days who helped their fathers, but in secret. Traditional Judaism does not allow women to touch the Torah. A horrible tradition, I know," he said. "But you really seem confident doing it and there's no reason you shouldn't continue, if you want the job."

I accepted. I earned $150 per day plus train fare and lunch, all of which was a lot for me at the time. My kids were in school, and I'd go to New York City once or twice a week to repair Torahs.

One day I was working on filling in some Hebrew letters. I had my period and had asked the scribe if it was all right for me to even be near the Torah, as more conservative sects of Judaism restrict what a menstruating woman is allowed to do. I remember Aunt Rose yelling, "Get away from the plants!" when I had my period. I knew that when we had "the curse" we were supposed to be tainted in some bullshit way. I didn't believe it, but I didn't want to get in trouble with the scribe either. He said, "What? Are you kidding?! It's fine," and that was the end of the conversation.

As I worked, I thought of how ironic it was that I was now practicing Judaism, that I was repairing a Torah, and on my period, no less. I wondered what my grandfather Joseph would have thought. Would he have been proud? Proud but horrified? I remembered him taking me to synagogue and how much it meant to him.

I started crying and I pushed myself away from the parchment of the Torah, because you can't get any water on it or it will damage it, and my tears would have stained it.

"What was I just working on?" I asked the scribe, as I don't really read Hebrew and can only identify a few letters.

"Oh," he said, running his finger along the line I had been filling in, "this is the part where Israel says to Joseph, 'Behold, I die: but God shall be with you, and bring you again to the land of your fathers'."

"Oh my God!" I said in disbelief, covered with goosebumps. I looked at the letters on the Torah scroll. "Joseph was my grandfather's name. I was just thinking of him, of what this would have meant to him."

The scribe smiled at me and said, "'Bring you again to the land of your fathers.' Freaky, right?"

I worked with the scribe for almost a year, but then the birth center was about to open, and I was becoming disillusioned with Torah repair.

More than once, there was a knock at the studio door and the scribe would look through the keyhole.

"Quick!" he'd whisper. "Get in the bathroom and stay there until I tell you it's okay to come out."

The first time I hid and waited, I could hear men's voices in the studio, and eventually I heard the front door open and close, and the studio became quiet again. The scribe knocked on the bathroom door and told me I could come out.

"What was that about?" I asked, annoyed but trying not to show it.

"Some Orthodox rabbis came to check on their Torah. They can't know a woman worked on it or it wouldn't be kosher."

"But...I AM working on it. Isn't that dishonest?"

"They don't need to know, and I can't afford to lose my jobs and referrals."

"Well, I think this religion stinks when it comes to how women are treated."

"You would not be wrong. But then again, look, women are rabbis now! That's progress!"

"Yes," I said, "but I was just told by a rabbi at the Jewish Theological Seminary, where the first female rabbi was ordained, that by working as a Torah scribe, I had DESECRATED the Torah. That I might as well have DEFECATED on it. That's progress? Please."

I was getting tired and angry about having to hide what I did. By the end of 1993, months after my daughter's bat mitzvah, no one in our family really wanted to go back to living Jewishly. Culturally, we were Jewish, yes, and wanted to keep some of the traditions, but as far as religion went, I found a lot wrong with Judaism. And I could understand why my very liberal mother had too.

I never quite knew how my mother learned to mother. I believe it was because she was brought up in a big, extended family where she was mothered not just by my grandmother Celia but by my great-aunt Sadie, my grandmother's sister. They all lived together on the farm in Mountaindale, and there were lots of kids around. My mother, being the second oldest child, was often in charge of caring for the younger ones.

My mother was affectionate. She sang to me and stroked my back, she let me take baths with her when I was very small, and she laughed when I was naughty, even when she didn't want to. Maybe I had something to do with that because my antics were sometimes outrageous. Once, she sent me to my room for some transgression and told me not to come out of my room for *any* reason until she said it was okay.

So, I took a petite dump on my bedroom floor, and lined up the three turds on my bookcase. When my mother finally opened my bedroom door, she exclaimed, "What the hell is that smell?" and began to laugh when I pointed to my production. She was trying not to, but to no avail. Granted this is the same Betty who saw fit to whip me with a belt for throwing my new shoes out the car window or when I got into her makeup and ruined her Avon lipstick and eyeshadow samples, but she and my father both dished out punishment with a belt. She was very different in personality from my father, but I think that kind of punishment was just what parents in their generation did.

I never whipped my kids. I remember once hitting my son with a wooden spoon when rage got the better of me, and once, after Miriam slapped me in the face with her sneaker, I slapped her right back with it. But my slap left tread marks and I was mortified. I regret every occasion that my temper got the better of me, whether I was angry verbally or physically. My physical anger was sometimes expressed on inanimate objects, like the night I threw a saucepan against the refrigerator door and shouted at the kids to make their own damn dinner. I dented the pan, and I was later embarrassed by my outburst. Yelling makes me cringe, even when I am the one doing the yelling.

Maybe it's because my parents punished me both verbally and physically. I always expect yelling to be followed by some sort of physical violence, whether a spanking or being whipped with a belt. This may have been the way people parented in the fifties and sixties, but it still had a huge and long-lasting impact.

To this day, if someone shouts at someone else, I want to dive under a table and cover my ears. If they raise their voice at me, I find myself barely able to ask the transgressor to please express themselves in a quieter voice, and I inevitably cry from the stress of it.

So, I was not like my mother when it came to punishing children. I was a believer in natural or logical consequences. Don't want to wear a coat to school in the winter? Okay, but you will see that you'll be cold. I would not argue or cajole or force my child to wear a coat, as my mother would have done. I would not require my kids to eat something they didn't like, the way my mother force fed me the same thing meal after meal until I finished it.

And while there was so much in her parenting that was

strict, there was still a kindness and gentleness there that I remember. Something that left for good when she died. After my mother was gone, there was a lack of softness in my world. No one stroked me or sang to me anymore, no one laughed good-naturedly at my pranks. I no longer had a cushion to protect me from the adults who threatened me. There was no protection from nuns or drunks in my bedroom or lecherous men. It was suddenly me fronting the world with no experience as to how to do it.

By the time I turned fifty, I knew what I wanted, if I lived. I wanted tenderness and kindness, I wanted to be strong in my independence and not frightened, and I wanted a companion who was a friend.

16

HUCKLEBERRY

I started to examine the kind of partner I would like in my life. Did I want to be with a man or a woman? Did I want another brother-sister relationship, like I had with Bill, or did I need wild passion? Would I stay in New York or was I willing to move? Did I want to—could I afford to—go home to California? Would anyone want me if they knew I had a brain injury? How obvious was it, anyway? How could I trust again, or did I never really trust anyone in the first place?

I decided that I wanted a passionate relationship with a man, that I would go anywhere to find it, that my brain injury was not obvious unless I was really tired, and I didn't have to share my health status at the beginning of a relationship. I realized that I had learned to trust my ex until he betrayed me, and I was pretty sure I could learn to trust again. More than anything, though, I wanted tenderness; tenderness like the kind my friend John offered me way back in our days at Irvine. Someone like John, I thought. Then it occurred to me that maybe I could find John himself.

I did an internet search for a man named John Beukema, and after a couple of false leads, I found who I thought was the right man living in Sacramento, California. I wrote him, asking if he had gone to UC Irvine, because if he had, there was something I wanted to tell him. I didn't realize that in wording that the way I did, John would read it and assume that he had fathered a child thirty years previously and would be quaking with trepidation. Once I clarified that he was not the father of our love child, I told him that the reason I was writing was to tell him something that I had never told him and that he might be happy to hear—that he was the most tender man I had ever met. He thanked me but said he didn't remember me, so I sent him a photo. "It rings bells," he said, "although not those of memory."

I explained that I used to show up at his apartment seeking a hug and consolation and that he always provided it. That we had hung out with Rick and Miranda and the Afghan puppies and swum naked. I reminded him of the friends we had in common, including my old roommate Lynn with whom he used to drop acid.

"Oh, I remember you now," he wrote. "You were the pest that used to hang out with us but wouldn't do drugs. A cute pest," he said.

"Yes to the no drugs," I said, "but I didn't think I was a pest. If you think I am now, I'll leave you alone."

But he didn't think I was a pest anymore, and he wanted to get to know me better, as an adult instead of the nineteen-year-old kid I was with him at Irvine. (He was five years older than me, and now we were fifty and fifty-five.) He was divorced, living alone, and was willing to travel and come to the Montreal Jazz Festival with me. John warned me that he was no longer as thin as he had been at Irvine and that he suffered from COPD (chronic obstructive pulmonary disease) and atrial fibrillation. He told me that in the nineties he had been busted for selling cocaine to an undercover agent in San Mateo County, California ("You idiot!" I wrote him), that he went to jail for a year and a half, and that was where he learned computer programming. That he'd dropped out of Irvine in his senior year, partially because he was suffering from PTSD following his time in the radio corps in Vietnam. That sometimes he smoked cigarettes.

If I had read all this on a dating profile or learned any of this about someone I was dating, I would have run fast and far. But this was John, the man who'd held me and soothed me when I was young. He couldn't be just his list of attributes; he used to be a good man and he deserved a chance, I told myself. I was excited and terrified to meet him again, with what-ifs spinning in my head. Little did I know then that I would fall deeply in love with him and he with me, the kind of love I had only read and dreamed about.

When I met him at the airport, as he stood there in his khaki shorts and Hawaiian shirt and Birkenstock sandals, I would not have recognized him had I not been searching for him at the gate. Then I saw his blue eyes, John's eyes. His ginger hair, now cut short. The round, rimless glasses. His freckles. His smile. And I smiled back.

After a day for John to recuperate from his flight, we

drove to the Montreal Jazz Festival, a five-hour drive from my house. My car was big and comfortable and air-conditioned, which shielded us from the blistering 106-degree heat. We shared intimate details about the lives we'd lived since UC Irvine and got to know each other better. Once in Montreal, we tried to withstand the heat, but it was miserable there. Our hotel's air conditioning was not working, and I was so sweaty I could not even peel my dress over my head to shower. John could barely breathe, or walk a block in the heat, so we decided to forego the rest of the festival and return to New York. On the ride home, John played some of his favorite CDs for me, including one of Richard Thompson, and I accused him of having white boy taste. I played the Bach Mass in B Minor that our choral group had recorded, and he listened in surprise.

"You have to promise to sing for me, or let me come to one of your concerts," he said. I was flattered and said I would. We talked for another five hours and got to know each other better still.

The next day I kissed him. We were sitting on my red couch, and I just leaned over and gave him the kind of kiss that I had never given him at Irvine and had not thought I would want to when I first saw him at the airport. But then I fell in love with him. I had hoped I would all along, until the inner monologue began, "What are you, crazy? Falling for a guy who could die on you at any minute? A CONVICT for God's sake! Are you nuts?" and then I tried to hold back on any intense feelings. I was unsuccessful.

The rest of his week with me was spent going out to eat, meeting my New York friends, sitting out on my back patio—me sunbathing naked in a lawn chair, once while smoking a cigar—gardening together, and talking and talking and talking. We discussed: God—he didn't believe, at the time I did; death—he was scared of it, so was I; family communication styles—his family had been silent and bottled up, mine had been loud and expressive; drugs —he was done with them, I was afraid of them still (except the legal ones I took for anxiety); kids—he didn't have any and wanted to meet mine, I didn't admit it but I was afraid of what my kids would think of him; jail—he'd deserved it, he said, I had never been inside one; brain injury—he was surprised to hear about mine, I felt comfortable sharing that I had one. There was sexual tension between us, and it crescendoed whenever we kissed, but that is all we did. I'd never been turned down before, especially not by someone who seemed so clearly attracted to me. I was confused, unsure about his feelings for me. But I was sure of mine.

As I kissed John goodbye at the terminal at LaGuardia on his way back to California, I told him I loved him. He did not reply in kind, and I spent the whole ride home berating myself for being foolish, for having blurted my feelings when they were not mutual. How could I have misinterpreted our kisses? That night and the next day were agony as I waited for an email from him. And he did write me, finally, to thank me for a wonderful week, and to tell me that he loved me too. That he had needed time to sort his feelings but once he had, and once he started missing me, he was sure of them. He loved me.

"Even though I am a pest?"

"Yes, but such an adorable, sexy pest."

"Good. We are going to have to explore just how sexy you think I am, though."

"Oh, I think we can arrange that. I still am carrying the image of you lying naked in that lawn chair smoking a cigar."

"Well hang on to that until I can give you some more images to carry."

"Believe me, I shall!"

John and I decided that we did not want to waste any time in getting together again. We wanted to spend the rest of our lives together, and we'd start in New York because I owned my house, and he rented his apartment. I flew to California to help him pack for the movers and meet his friends in Sacramento and San Francisco. And he'd meet mine in Los Angeles. We'd say goodbye to our friends, then we'd fly home to New York.

In Sacramento, in his studio apartment, we explored all the feelings we had for each other, and I experienced the most passionate, abandoned lovemaking I ever had in my life. Practically every time I came with John I would cry I was so filled with emotion. And talk about trust! John had a pair of sheepskin-lined handcuffs that I allowed him to use on me. It was possibly the best sex I have ever had, relinquishing control and letting John guide me to heights of ecstasy. It sounds trite, but it's true. After being raped in college, I could never really let go when I made love to anyone, except my husband. With John, it was a different, deeper kind of letting go.

One day, on our drive back from San Francisco to Sacramento, I told John that I knew how to cook pozole, Mexican pork stew with red chiles. He picked up my left hand and slid an imaginary ring down my ring finger.

"What was that?" I asked. "You're proposing to me because I can cook pozole?"

"You bet," he said.

"Really?"

"Really."

"So, how do you imagine that happening?" I asked.

"We'll have a party for our friends back in New York, and your kids will be there, and maybe my friend Pete from San Francisco, and a justice of the peace will show up, and they'll marry us."

"I like that idea," I said.

"So, that's a yes?"

"That's a yes."

The day the movers came, John and I stood alone in his empty Sacramento apartment, him behind me with his hands on my shoulders, looking at the Anna's humming-bird sitting quietly on a sycamore branch outside his balcony.

On our way home, my fear of flying reappeared and John needed to reassure me that we wouldn't die in flight. He took my hand, stroked my face, and explained Bernoulli's principle to me, how the airflow over the top of the plane moved slower than the airflow under the plane so that if it was in forward motion, a plane had to fly, it couldn't not. When I said that I hated takeoff, that that was the part that scared me, he said that was his favorite part.

"Think of it like being in a turbocharged convertible full of blonds!"

"I'm sorry but the imagery does not work for me, except maybe the turbocharged part."

"Then think of that," he said, "and I'll hold your hand."

As the plane took off, I was pale with fear and John squeezed my hand and grinned at me.

"And think of the life we are going to have together, Julietta! It's going to be wonderful." Upon which he kissed me, my first airplane kiss.

Back in New York, we were invited by some of my friends to observe Yom Kippur, the Jewish Day of Atonement. John's mother was the daughter of a Czech Jewish mother, which made her Jewish even if she never acknowledged her Jewish roots. And by the laws of matrilinear Judaism, John was thus also Jewish and wanted to celebrate Jewish holidays with me. We decided to attend Kol Nidre services the night before Yom Kippur and attend a breakfast after sundown on Yom Kippur.

As we prepared to go to Kol Nidre services, I joined John in the bathroom where he was showering.

"John, I have no idea what the words Kol Nidre mean," I said, "I just know it's the night before Yom Kippur, when we are supposed to atone for our sins. And fast all day, which I am not doing."

"Oh, I looked it up," said John. "Kol Nidre means 'All Vows,' and it's when Jews make their vows to God."

"Who you don't believe in. What vows did you make?"

John pulled the shower curtain aside. He had shampoo in his hair.

"I vow to love you for the rest of my life," he said.

I leaned in to kiss him.

"I vow to love you, too," I said.

"I'm your Huckleberry," he said with a grin, quoting the film *Tombstone*, where Val Kilmer utters those words. It means "I'm the man for the job."

Two days later, September 17, 2002, it was beautiful and sunny. The sky was cerulean blue, the leaves were still green on the trees, but a few dried brown ones had fallen to the ground. I was inside on the desktop computer, chatting with a friend in Boston via AOL Instant Messenger. John was outside pulling weeds in the garden and had said he wanted to rake leaves, even though I told him it was too early in the season and that I had someone to do it.

That morning John had rented a post office box in Bedford Hills and had opened a bank account in Mount Kisco. He'd made an appointment with a cardiologist for October 7, 2002, because he didn't trust his cardiologist in Sacramento. He had started to look at the want ads for jobs as a programmer specializing in credit card verification, and we were thrilled to see that the salaries for those jobs was upwards of $180,000 per year. We talked about enlarging my little cottage so there were two bathrooms and office space for both of us and had even gone on walks in the neighborhood to see what other people had built to make their cottages bigger. We agreed on style and had started making rough sketches (John had wanted to be an architect).

Our life together was falling into a kind of rhythm. I had gotten so comfortable with him that I had even said, that very morning before he left for town, "I could really use some alone time in my own house." It felt like a normal thing to say to a partner if one were being honest. We had spent thirty-two days together, 24/7, and I think we both appreciated the break.

"You're going to have to kiss me goodbye though," said John, "if you really want me to leave."

He lifted me onto the kitchen counter, where I sat with my legs around his waist. We began to kiss passionately, but then he stopped.

"We are going to continue this later!" he said. "Be prepared."

"Oh, I am, honey. Don't you worry."

As the afternoon shadows grew longer, and I was typing away to my Boston friend telling her how happy and in love I was, I noticed I no longer heard the rake scraping through the grass and on the driveway.

"You know," I typed to my friend, "John's been back for over an hour, and I still haven't seen him. I need to go make sure that I haven't chased him away."

I walked down my front steps and saw John's feet sticking out of my garage door.

"What did you do, die on me?" I joked. "I didn't need THAT much space," I said, as I rounded the side of the garage.

And there John lay, on his back, eyes open, rake across his chest, with berry-sized patches mottling his body. At first, I wasn't sure he was dead. Then I realized his eyes were fixed and open, and if he'd been napping they would have been closed. And why would he nap on the garage floor? And weren't those spots on his body signs of death? These thoughts raced through my mind in milliseconds, and then I began to scream. I ran into the house, grabbed the phone, and called 911. Then I returned to John and knelt over him, my hands spread wide on his broad chest.

"Oh, NOOOOOOOOOOOOOO! NO! NO! NO!" I shouted and sobbed. Neighbors collected in the driveway. I overheard Ellen (who lived two doors down from my house) telling someone that she thought she heard a coyote howling until she realized it was a person and the sound was coming from my house. She ran over to join the crowd amassing in my driveway, to rub my back and comfort me.

I was blind with shock and grief and don't remember all the details of that afternoon. I know the ambulance arrived and they hoisted John onto a stretcher but did not cover his face with a sheet, so I still hoped he was alive even though I knew better. I know that two friends drove me to the emergency room and sat with me, waiting for the doctor to come out. I remember Ellen showing up at the ER with Maalox because I had horrible stomach pains and the hospital could not give me anything as I was not the patient. I remember the doctor, named Dr. Newborn, coming to me, shaking his head, and saying "I'm sorry, there was nothing we could do."

I was allowed to go in and see John, whose body was still slightly warm and who was covered in a blanket, with eyes closed as if he were sleeping. I buried my face in his hair and breathed deeply, kissing his head, and telling him, "I love you, Huckleberry."

Miraculously, when I got home, my house was filled with people I loved. There was my daughter, Miriam, who seemed to have teleported from university in Philadelphia. My closest friends were there. All I could do was sit on my couch and sob so hard I got a migraine. Calls had been made to John's sister and brother, in Boston and San Diego, to come to New York and within a day they appeared. My choir director tore open my front door and rushed in to hug me. Some people stayed at my house, others came and went. For two days I didn't have to do anything to take care of myself, as tea or food suddenly appeared. I suspect it was Miriam running the household.

What was so different to me between John's death and my mother's death is that when John died, I didn't feel out of control. I was in touch with the coroner, who told me

John had died instantly of a heart attack and was probably dead before he hit the ground. My friends Sheri and Kathy, members of my Pussy Posse, were by my side almost the whole time, and my friend Pam, another Pussy Posse member, showed up with, and planted, a cherry tree in John's honor on my front lawn. I had support from everyone and was never alone. I handled the funeral arrangements (he was cremated) and arranged a memorial for him at my house.

The rabbi we called refused to do a service for John because he didn't know him and because John hadn't been raised Jewish, despite his mother having technically been a Jew. I decided on my eloquent, loving friend Isaac, who had been on my birth center board (and for whom Bill and I had been role models as parents) to lead a service. John's sister, Miriam, and I decided on poems to be read at the memorial, including the Gerard Manley Hopkins poem "Pied Beauty" for our freckled man, which he would have hated for the God references but was nevertheless beautiful, as were John's freckles to me. And my friend Michael Boriskin, a classical pianist, played a Brahms lullaby on an electric piano set up on the lawn. Some members of my choir sang a beautiful piece which I can't remember. I sang too, as I'd promised my Huckleberry I would. Mostly I sobbed, and whenever I did my son Noah did too. My friend Ann, the last member of the Pussy Posse, had to ask the Good Humor Man to stop playing "It's a Small World" as he drove around the neighborhood. That gave me my first laugh in days. John would have found it very amusing too.

We scattered some of John's ashes into the hole around the cherry tree. John's friend Pete, who'd come from California, took some ashes home to be scattered by private plane over Drakes Bay in John's favorite city, San Francisco. John's brother took some home to put in an urn in San Diego. I took some ashes to Mystic, Connecticut, and later to Havana, Cuba, and scattered them there. By now, John's ashes have probably met each other coming and going. He's gotten to do the traveling he always wished he could.

The weeks following John's death were heavy and depressing. I couldn't eat. I didn't want to shower or dress. I'd break down sobbing at random times. But it was adult anguish, the kind you can wrap your head around with soothing words and cognition of things like Kübler-Ross' five stages of grief, and know that, in time, the intensity of feelings would pass. This journey back to normalcy was going to be a motherfucker, but I wasn't alone on it. Unlike when my mother died, I was not abandoned or ignored. I had friends on both coasts checking in on me, I had a therapist, I had a bereavement support group, I was palpably loved. I knew I would heal, eventually.

I don't regret falling in love with John. It was the first time in my life that I felt loved unreservedly, and I experienced the same in return. I didn't feel impatient with or critical of him, and I respected the hell out of him. At the memorial, as some of my friends spoke, Kathy and Pete had a sweet argument over who was smarter, me or John. And they both agreed that we had been perfect for each other with very compatible intellects. I will miss John for the rest of my life, and every September 17 I feel a twinge of deep hurt. I cry often when I remember his loving touch. If I try really hard, I can still feel his hands on my shoulders, the relaxed way we were with each, the tenderness. Whenever I see a hummingbird, I think of him.

I am grateful to have had the opportunity to know such love, and feel such love for someone, and to know what to look for in the future. And to know that there is a future, even without him.

17

KAVVANAH

"Allow yourself to sit or lie down in a comfortable position, noticing how your body feels, where there might be tension. And when you're ready, allow your eyes to close, and take some easy, letting-go breaths," I spoke softly and slowly to my pregnant client, looking back at me through the computer screen. Zoom became the way I saw so many of my clients when the pandemic upended our lives.

"I'm legitimately terrified," Melody said, on the verge of tears, trying to find a place of calm amidst the anxiety. She had an intense needle phobia, one that had caused her to faint and have convulsions. "What if I faint? If they need to draw blood, or if I need an IV? What if I faint *in* labor?"

"As if! People would *pay* to be able to faint in labor and wake up done with the whole thing!" She laughed a little, and I continued. "To the best of my knowledge that has never, ever happened. And I also think you are strong and capable of doing this. You are going to be okay."

With a hand on her belly, Melody took a deep breath

and settled back into her chair as we continued the hypnosis session.

It's been almost twenty years since John's death. The birth center closed in 2004, ten years after it opened, due to hospital mismanagement. While I've continued to be a birth doula and childbirth educator, I also became a certified hypnotherapist, specializing in anxiety and pain management, working predominantly with pregnant people. I wanted to expand my reach so that I could help people feel their power *before* they gave birth, enabling them to feel safe in their bodies and go with the flow of pregnancy, labor, and delivery.

Melody and I worked, in successive sessions, on relaxation, fear release, grounding, and numbing sensation. Then we culminated our work in imagining a birth in which she was calm and confident. Which is exactly what she had when the day came. She had a great birth with no fear of needles and no fainting. She thanked me profusely for helping her, and, to be honest, I was a little surprised when I heard that I had been successful. But after her first blood draw and no fainting, and then after her birth, I knew my techniques were effective, and I felt pride in the work that I do. I've subsequently worked with several people who had needle phobias, and I've helped all of them.

There are days when I feel great success in my work and others when I feel like I have not done nearly enough to impact women's lives.

When I have those doubts, I pull out the letter that I got from my colleague Jemima fifteen years ago, who at the time was also a birth doula.

· · ·

Julietta,

 I wanted to thank you last night at the Hudson Valley Birth Network meeting, but I am shy in groups. I appreciate all the work that you did to open The Birth Cottage. Last night a few people said how The Birth Cottage influenced them, and it influenced me too. I had my first baby there. I didn't know anything about birth, only that I didn't want a needle in my back, and I believed that my body knew how to give birth without medical interventions. I left my OB because I didn't like how I was treated. I always left his office feeling judged. I found out about the midwives who worked out of The Birth Cottage, and I fell in love with them. I fell in love with The Birth Cottage.

 During my baby's birth I was totally relaxed, the atmosphere was so welcoming and calming, and the midwife was completely focused on me. Even though my daughter's birth was long, I left The Birth Cottage amazed at what I could do. I adored being in labor and giving birth. I wanted to be around birth for the rest of my life. If The Birth Cottage hadn't existed, I doubt that I would ever have become a doula, let alone have more children.

 So, truly, thank you. Your work in achieving your dream helped me achieve mine.

 Jemima

Today Jemima is a midwife, creating sacred spaces for people to birth in. Her work continues the kavvanah, the direction of the heart, that she and I and countless others practice in order to keep birth holy and safe. For us, choosing to become a mother is a political act that empowers and strengthens people, exhausting as it is sometimes.

 One way to overcome the disparities that exist in

maternal health today is to teach pregnant people to use their voices, to demand that they be treated with respect, or, like me and Jemima, find other providers who will listen to us and give us that respect. And, like me and Jemima, they might increase their power exponentially by going on to influence other pregnant people.

I am honored to have been part of a group of people worldwide who fought hard to change the birthing landscape. In nearly every community now there are midwives, home birth practices, birthing centers, and hospitals offering a much different kind of birth experience than in the 1970s. Partners are welcomed now, as are birth doulas. People can have joyful births without fear, and they are supported by large communities of postpartum doulas and lactation consultants through pregnancy, birth, and the fourth trimester.

How I have managed to find my place in the world inspiring mothers when I was a motherless child used to be a mystery to me. I felt the need to make up for what I didn't have, a corrective life if you will. I'm not sure that I was always the most patient, creative, attentive mother, but I passionately chose motherhood, and I love my children and grandchildren fiercely and protectively.

Last fall, when the sky was a clear, bright blue and the maple leaves were fluttering in golden radiance in Brooklyn's Prospect Park, I went for a walk there with my daughter, who had her infant daughter, Silvia, in front of her in a baby carrier. The light slanted in just such a way that for a moment Miriam looked like my mother. There are times when she radiates my mother's authoritative confidence and has a certain look in her dark eyes that causes me to catch my breath, as if I am seeing a specter. My mother would have loved Miriam, who makes herbal remedies and tinctures and salves, and eats only organic food. She is consummately Betty's granddaughter. And consummately my daughter. Miriam had both her babies at home and is an amazing mother, balancing a career and motherhood in a way I think my mother would have enjoyed if given the choice.

On a personal level, my work is done. The matrilineal threads have been braided from my grandmother Celia to my mother, Betty, to me to my daughter, Miriam, and now my granddaughter, Silvia. And I am content.

EPILOGUE

On a political level, my work will never end. Unfortunately, the United States ranks last in maternal mortality among industrialized nations, disproportionately impacting Black pregnant people. The countries with the best outcomes have the midwifery model of care for their low-risk birthing people, and yet in the United States less than 10% of babies are born with the help of midwives. That is a reality that saddens and infuriates me because within our reach we have the ability to create change, yet we are blocked by the powerful lobbies of doctors and hospitals, who try to frighten pregnant people into believing that pregnancy, labor, and birth are medical emergencies that need to be managed.

The World Health Organization has long considered the ideal rate for cesarean births to be between 10% and 15%, yet according to the March of Dimes, the cesarean rate is closer to 32%, and in my neck of the woods (Westchester County, New York) some hospitals have cesarean rates over 50%. Almost all people who have had a cesarean birth believed they needed an "emergency" cesarean and cite the reasons the doctor gave them for performing surgical birth. Yet rarely was the need to operate an emergency; rather it was a matter of convenience for the medical provider who could not patiently wait, or it was the need of the terrified pregnant person to be relieved of their fears in whatever way possible. If my mother had had access to better options, I would never have been born through surgical intervention. She would have chosen a childbirth center, just like I did. Because of the work that people like Jemima and I do across the United States, people like my daughter have had the knowledge and support to give birth safely and at home on their own terms.

As this book goes to press, reproductive rights are in a very precarious place—the history of the United States is going backwards. For fifty years, I fought for, advocated for, and supported reproductive freedom. And with this plethora of anti-choice legislation comes details eerily familiar to me. People are being watched, hotlines set up to call and report suspicious activity, rewards for turning people in. It's McCarthyism all over again just wearing a new dress. Subversive. A threat. Unmotherly.

Every time I see someone take control of their birth choices, no matter what those are, I know all the hard work I have done, and continue to do, has been worth it.

PHOTOS

My mother, Betty Raskin Appleton, in her New York office at the Betty Raskin Agency, 489 Fifth Avenue, in the early 1940s.

Me and my mother at home on Durant Drive in Beverly Hills, 1952.

Me and my father in Los Angeles, 1953.

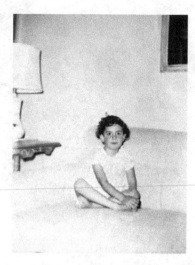

At home on Sarah Street in Studio City, California, age four, 1956.

My fifth birthday, 1957. L to R: Grandpa Joseph and Grandma Celia, cousin Steven, me, my mother, Aunt Pearl, cousin Janis, and Uncle Alfred.

At home with my mother and my father, 1958.

My mother, Aunt Clara, Uncle Harry, and me.

Me in my Girl Scout uniform in 1961, the year my mother died.

Me with my neighbor and babysitter, Marge, on Sarah Street, 1963, after my mother died and right before we left for Europe.

At Bibione Beach in Bibione, Italy, 1963.

At school in Ibiza, Spain, 1964.

Me on far left at my twelfth birthday party in Ibiza,
February 29, 1964.

On the Johnsons' rooftop in Telde, Gran Canaria,
December 1964.

In London with my new coat from Harrods, 1965.

Dinner aboard the ship from Las Palmas to England,
December 1965.

On the ship back to the States via the Panama Canal,
1965.

Modeling for art classes, 1972.

In labor with Noah in Los Angeles, 1978.

Me and Noah visiting my father in Laguna Hills, California, 1978.

With Noah, age four, and Miriam, age one, in Cape Cod, 1982.

Mother's Day in Noank, Connecticut, 1989.

Unhappily married, 1995.

Me and John in Los Angeles, 2002.

Reny and me in San Francisco, 2005.

With my granddaughter in Brooklyn, 2021.

With my grandson in New York, 2016.

At work as a doula in Norfolk, Virginia, 2015. (Photo credit: Ash and Bean Photography)

Visiting friends in Cadiz, Spain, 2016.

ACKNOWLEDGMENTS

Thank you to my first readers, beloved friends, editors, and publishers: Isaac Brooks, Karen Delshad, Kim Ellis, Neville Frankel, Stuart Friedman, Gloria Gorell, Shari Harris, Diane Ingalls, Babette Kronstadt, Aimee Tanizaki Kurland, Elizabeth Rosen Mayer, Dena Oppenheim, Susan Raab, Isabel Rachlin, Jeff Rachlin, Ellen Rubin, Alexandra Asher Sears, Morgan Schechter Shanahan, Andy Sholl, Steve Sholl, Eric Stand, Georgann Stewart, and Miranda Wicker. You believed I could write, and I hope I did you proud.

For the gorgeous cover, thank you to my friend Reny Mia Slay. To Noah and Miriam, thank you for letting me practice mothering on you. And thank you to my grandson, Charlie, for teaching me to be a grandmother. Bibi loves you.

ABOUT THE AUTHOR

Julietta Appleton is the founder and former director of The Birth Cottage, the first freestanding birth center in Westchester County, New York. She co-founded the Hudson Valley Birth Network and one of Montreal's first rape crisis centers. Her writing credits include the books *Clothing Optional* and *Journey to Parenthood*, and she served as editor for *Spinning Babies' Breech Birth Quick Guide* and *Spinning Babies' Quick Reference Booklet*. In addition, Julietta has written columns for the Westchester County *Record-Review*, *Lewisboro Ledger*, *Westchester Magazine*, and *Fairfield Magazine* and has translated the diaries of Frida Kahlo and writings of Cuban dissidents. Through her work as a childbirth educator and certified hypnotherapist, Julietta has helped people overcome their fears and limiting beliefs, guiding them to create positive change and achieve their goals. She lives in New York and continues to be a fierce midwifery advocate.